FSC
www.fsc.org
MIX
Papier | Fördert gute Waldnutzung
FSC® C083411

Kolibri 360 GmbH
Ferdinand-Jühlke-Straße 7
99095 Erfurt, Deutschland
produktsicherheit@kolibri360.de

The Sacred Sound Path

Walking with Nāda Brahma and My Guru

The Sacred Sound Path

Walking with Nāda Brahma and My Guru

P. Sesh Kumar

THE BROWSER

Title: The Sacred Sound Path:
Walking with Nāda Brahma and My Guru
Author: P. Sesh Kumar

ISBN: 978-93-49042-84-1

Published by:
JGS Enterprises Pvt Ltd
Imprint: The Browser

Publisher's Address:
SCO 14-15, FF, Sector 8-C, Chandigarh 160 009

Website: thebrowser.org
Email: service@thebrowser.org

THE BROWSER
Publishers & Booksellers

Contents

Acknowledgements

Writing this book has been a journey of the heart, a labor of love, and above all, a humble offering at the lotus feet of my revered Guru, Parama Pujya Sri Ganapathy Sachchidananda Swamiji. His divine presence, boundless compassion, and transformative music have been the guiding light in my life, illuminating paths I never imagined and instilling in me a profound sense of purpose and devotion.

I extend my deepest gratitude to Pujya Sri Datta Vijayananda Teertha Swamiji, the Uttaradhikari of Avadhoota Datta Peetham, whose wisdom, humility, and spiritual leadership continue to inspire countless devotees, including myself. His blessings have been a source of strength throughout this endeavor.

I would fail in my duty if I do not profusely thank Sri H.V. Prasad, Executive Trustee of Avadhoota Datta Peetham, whose unwavering support and encouragement have been instrumental in bringing this work to fruition. His dedication to the mission of the Peetham and his personal guidance have been invaluable.

To my beloved wife, Usha, and our sons, Anirudh and Datta Ganesh, along with our daughters-in-law, Deepika and Saloni, I express my deepest appreciation for their unwavering support, patience, and understanding during the time I was immersed in writing this book. Their love and encouragement have been the bedrock of my journey.

I am also profoundly grateful to my dear friends, Mr. Manish Anand and Mr. Pankaj Singh, whose extraordinary dedication and support were pivotal in the timely publication of this book. Their commitment and hard work ensured that this labor of love reached the hands of readers without delay.

This book is not merely a collection of words but a testament to the transformative power of divine grace, the healing essence of sacred sound, and the boundless compassion of a living Master. It is my sincere hope that it serves as a bridge for seekers, guiding them toward the inner stillness and joy that Sri Swamiji so lovingly embodies.

With humility and devotion, I offer this work at the sacred feet of my Guru, Parama Pujya Sri Ganapathy Sachchidananda Swamiji.

—P. Sesh Kumar
March 2025

Preface

My Journey With Nāda Brahma[1] *Pujya Sri Ganapathy Sachchidananda Swamiji*

How do you begin to describe someone who lives beyond description? How do you capture, in mere words, a life that radiates silence, compassion, cosmic sound, and transformation? How does one write about a saint who heals not just through His hands or words but through vibrations, breath, trees, birds, and song?

---

1. Nāda Brahma is a Sanskrit phrase that means 'Sound is God' or 'The Divine is Sound'. It comes from ancient Indian philosophy, especially from the Vedas and spiritual texts related to music and yoga.

In simple English, Nāda Brahma means that the entire universe is made of vibrations or sound, and these vibrations are sacred. Everything we see, feel, or experience—including our thoughts and emotions—is a form of vibration. Music, especially spiritual music, is a way to connect with this universal energy or God. Just like a temple or a prayer, sound can take us closer to the divine.

Sri Ganapathy Sachchidananda Swamiji often uses this concept in His Music for Meditation and Healing, where ragas (musical scales) are used not just to entertain but to heal and elevate the soul—because sound, in its pure form, is a pathway to God.

That is the impossible task I found myself facing when I set out to write this book on Pujya Sri Ganapathy Sachchidananda Swamiji—spiritual master, Avadhoota, Nāda Yogi, healer, mystic, and global torchbearer of Sanatana Dharma.

But this book is not a biography in the conventional sense. It is a journey—through music, miracles, mysticism, healing, silence, and self-discovery. It is the story of one person's transformation—from a rationalist civil servant to a seeker, a believer, a witness—and it is also the story of how one divine life continues to touch millions across the globe, cutting across religions, cultures, borders, and belief systems.

I come from the Indian Audit and Accounts Service (IAAS), a world of numbers, facts, and verifiable truths. For decades, my life revolved around audits and accounts, logic and law. And yet, for over 33 years, I have been quietly journeying through another reality—one governed not by rationality but by divine resonance, not by rulebooks but by soul books.

In Chapter 1, we begin with the obvious but impossible question—Who is Sri Ganapathy Sachchidananda Swamiji? Born under mystical circumstances, raised by a divine mother, and walking a path of silent inner mastery from childhood, Sri Swamiji's early life set the stage for a mission that would blend ancient wisdom with modern outreach.

Chapter 2 offers a personal lens into this divine encounter. As someone who had never set foot between 1986 and 1989 in His Ashram despite multiple visits to Mysuru, I recount how a series of 'coincidences'—beginning with bhajan cassettes in remote Nagaland—led me to Sri Swamiji and transformed my life. Chapter 6 continues this personal journey, touching upon miracles that are too precise to be dismissed and too frequent to be denied.

Then comes Chapter 3, which dives into the heart of Sri Swamiji's mission: Nāda Brahma—the sacred sound as divine presence. Here, we explore how sound, in its purest form, becomes a vehicle for awakening and healing and how Sri Swamiji's concerts are not performances but transmissions of divine frequency.

Chapter 4 brings together science and spirituality as we explore how modern neuroscience (drawing on Daniel J. Levitin's research) validates the ancient Indian understanding of Nāda Chikitsa, or healing through sound. Sri Swamiji's Raga Ragini Vidya—his magnum opus—stands as a bridge between Eastern metaphysics and Western medicine.

Chapter 5 builds on this theme by revisiting a now-classic article from 2006 by Bill Osmer. His observations offer rare insights into how Sri Swamiji's music bypasses the intellect and touches the soul, often inducing stillness, healing, or deep meditation without a word being spoken.

In Chapter 7, we trace Sri Swamiji's spiritual lineage—the eternal flame of the Guru Parampara, rooted in Bhagawan Dattatreya and carried forth through the Avadhoota tradition. His own life stands as a living testament to this timeless legacy, radiating the power of inner silence, detachment, and wisdom-in-action.

Chapters 8 and 9 offer a deep dive into Datta Kriya Yoga, the unique breath-based spiritual practice given by Sri Swamiji for inner balance and well-being. We also compare it with modern yoga systems, revealing how ancient prana-based methods offer far more than mere physical fitness—they unlock inner alchemy.

Chapter 10 turns to the sacred music of Sri Swamiji—not just as art but as living soundscapes that heal and uplift. His 3,000+ bhajans in multiple languages are more than devotional songs; they are vibrational maps of consciousness that guide the listener inward.

From there, we shift to a topic close to Sri Swamiji's heart—eco-spirituality. In Chapter 11, we walk through the

Kishkindha Moolika Bonsai Garden and Shuka Vana, both vibrant expressions of His love for nature, silence, and the interconnectedness of all life.

Chapter 12 returns to philosophy and metaphysics, exploring the Avadhoota lineage of Dattatreya and the significance of Sri Swamiji's mission in this unbroken spiritual tradition—where God is both immanent and transcendent, both playful and profound.

The global impact of His work comes into sharp focus in Chapter 13, where we reflect on mass recitations of Hanuman Chalisa, Bhagavad Gita and sacred mantras organized by Sri Swamiji to invoke collective peace and spiritual unity. With Guinness World Records and unprecedented gatherings, these events show how ancient mantras and shlokas continue to shape our modern world.

Chapter 14 touches a tender chord—the empowerment of the differently-abled. Sri Swamiji's initiatives for inclusivity and compassion, especially for children with developmental challenges, reflect His view that every soul is divine, regardless of physical or mental limitations.

Chapter 15 explores Sri Swamiji's global network of Datta Temples and Ashrams, from Mysuru to Trinidad and from London to Baton Rouge. Each one is not merely a structure—it is a sacred battery of healing, devotion, and unity.

And finally comes Chapter 16, where we enter the realm of the Miracle of Manifestation. From mass chantings that electrify continents to Gita recitations on sacred soil, from the architectural marvel of the Nāda Mandapa to the swift and sublime consecration of the Datta Venkateshwara Temple—these events and creations defy logic. They were not merely planned. They were manifested through divine sankalpa, clarity of vision, and a level of execution that can only be called sacred. The 70-foot tall Karya Siddhi Hanuman, the laser show, the flawless acoustics of Nāda Mandapa, the spiritual gravitas of

Kurukshetra recitations—each project, each moment, reflects a higher orchestration. Time and again, what should have taken years was completed in months. What seemed impossible was achieved without friction. Faith flowed faster than funds. Volunteers rose above their limitations. Officials delivered the impossible. Why? Because this was not construction—it was consecration.

Sri Swamiji did not just inspire action. He created momentum—a rhythm of sacred will that infected every devotee, every organizer, every spectator. This was not project management—it was a divine manifestation. And those who participated in it, even in the smallest way, became part of living history.

Why did I write this book?

Because it had to be written.

Because the world needs to know—not just about Sri Swamiji, the spiritual Master but also Sri Swamiji, the healer, the revolutionary musician, the seer-scientist of sound, and the global ambassador of inner peace.

Because in an age of anxiety, distraction, and disconnection, His music speaks directly to the soul—without any translation, without any preconditions.

Because His life is the living embodiment of Nāda Brahma—the sacred truth that Sound is God and that healing, joy, and self-realization are all just one divine note away.

Because what I experienced in Sri Swamiji's presence—what I have witnessed and what I continue to discover—is too precious not to share. Because we live in a time when the world needs healing, stillness, and connection. And this book, I hope, is a small offering toward that cause.

It is my humble attempt to introduce the reader to a Master who doesn't just speak about divinity—He sings it, breathes it, plays it, heals with it, and embodies it.

This is not just a book. It is an invitation.

To listen. To breathe. To reflect.

To let sound lead you inward.

To see the sacred in the silence.

And to know that in this noisy world, there exists still the music of the soul—flowing from a Master who is, in truth and in essence, Nāda Brahma.

To listen—not just to music, but to the inner silence that follows it. To the healing that arises when sound and soul meet. And perhaps, if grace permits, to hear the most subtle of all sounds—the Anahata Nāda,[2] the unstruck sound that Sri Swamiji transmits not just through His music but through His very presence.

I write not as a scholar or saint but as a humble devotee, attempting to capture in words a life that continues to defy words.

This book is my offering, at the feet of a Master whose life has become a living raga of compassion, clarity, courage, and cosmic sound.

May it serve, in some small way, as a bridge—for those who are seeking, suffering, or simply curious—to walk toward the healing light that is Sri Ganapathy Sachchidananda Swamiji.

—P. Sesh Kumar,
March 2025

---

2. Anahata Nāda is a subtle, inner sound that arises without any external vibration or physical contact, perceived in deep meditation. It is considered a divine, eternal vibration symbolizing the cosmic sound of OM, resonating from the heart centre (Anahata Chakra) and leading the seeker inward toward spiritual realization.

CHAPTER 1

Who is Sri Ganapathy Sachchidananda Swamiji?

How does one describe, say, the Sun? Or even the Moon? Or the Sky? That is 'One,' Who cannot be described or explained in words or in written material or through any of the five known human senses. This is not the only dilemma. The other conundrum is that there are a number of books, websites, and articles written by eminent persons and longstanding devotees across the world highlighting their intense and miraculous experiences in the association of Paramapujya Sri Ganapathy Sachchidananda Swamiji. So, what additional value would I be able to add to the existing and available literature on Paramapujya Sri Swamiji?

I craved His blessings before I began this venture. The blessings came readily, instructing that I complete the book at the earliest. I, therefore, proceed invoking His blessings.

Having taken a human form, Sri Swamiji has had to endure all the unimaginable physical discomforts and penury right from childhood, besides having been deprived of the nurturing presence of His mother—the Guru and mother rolled into one, at a crucial stage in His childhood. Born on May 26,

1942, at the sacred confluence of the Arkavati and Kaveri rivers in Mekedatu, Karnataka, Sri Ganapathy Sachchidananda Swamiji emerged as a beacon of spiritual enlightenment. His birth, enveloped in mystical significance, was foretold to His parents, Sri Narasimha Sastry and Sri Jaya Lakshmi Mata,[3] by a Hindu saint and a Moslem fakir both of whom predicted the child's destiny to possess supreme wisdom and uplift humanity. Remarkably, He was born on a rock in the Kaveri River, with His mother in deep meditation and the newborn covered in holy ash.

From a tender age, Sri Swamiji exhibited profound spiritual inclinations, organizing satsangs and teaching bhajans to His peers. His innate ability to perceive individuals' past, present, and future allowed Him to guide many through their tribulations. In 1966, He established the Mysuru Ashram,[4] now known as Avadhoota Datta Peetham or Sri Ganapathy Sachchidananda Swamiji Ashram, on Ooty Road, initially a modest straw hut, which became the foundation of the Avadhoota Datta Peetham. This institution is dedicated to preserving and propagating ancient Vedic traditions and practices.

---

3. Sri Jayalakshmi Mata, the revered mother and Guru of Sri Ganapathy Sachchidananda Swamiji, played a foundational role in shaping His divine mission and spiritual destiny. As a realized soul, she awakened Sri Swamiji's latent spiritual powers from childhood and initiated Him into deep yogic practices and divine knowledge. Her divine presence and guidance continue to inspire and protect the Datta lineage, with Sri Swamiji often referring to her as the eternal guiding force behind His life and work.

4. Sri Ganapathy Sachchidananda Swamiji has established numerous ashrams, temples, and Datta Yoga Centers worldwide. For a comprehensive and up-to-date list of these centers, including their addresses and contact information, please refer to the official website of Avadhoota Datta Peetham: https://www.dattapeetham.org/ashramcenters. This resource provides detailed information on all the centers associated with Sri Swamiji's mission across India and internationally.

A prolific composer, Sri Swamiji has penned over 3,000 bhajans or keertanas in Sanskrit, Kannada, Telugu, and Hindi, captivating both laypersons and scholars with his enthralling sessions. His literary works, including the pioneering research study Raga Ragini Nāda Yoga[5] for which Sri Swamiji was awarded honorary doctorate by Sri Krishnadevaraya University, Bellary, Karnataka, 'Sachchidananda Neeti Mala,' 'Chutuku Sahitya,' and 'Vedanta Geetalu,' discourses on Bhagavatam, Mahabharata, and Ramayana, serve as guiding lights for seekers. Equally significant are His discourses since compiled into publications on *Guru Gita,*[6] *Avadhoota Gita*, and *Datta Darshana*, to name a few.

Sri Swamiji's humanitarian efforts are vast and varied. He has inspired the establishment of educational institutions, initiated relief programs for the underprivileged, and championed Annadanam (food distribution) globally. His environmental contributions are notable, with the creation of the Kishkindha Moolika Bonsai Garden, housing over 2,600 meticulously shaped miniature trees, and Shuka Vana,[7] an aviary that shelters more than 2,000 birds representing 486 species.

His endeavors have earned him multiple Guinness World Records, including leading 1,28,918 participants in the chanting of the Hanuman Chalisa in Tenali, Andhra Pradesh, on January 31, 2015, and conducting the largest music therapy lesson with 1,814 participants at the Sydney Opera House on April 6, 2015. Additionally, he achieved records for the

5. Discussed in later chapters.

6. *Guru Gita* or the 'song of the guru', is a Hindu scripture comprising a dialogue between Shiva and Parvati, wherein the former expounds on the significance of the guru in spiritual practice. This text, part of Skanda Purana, emphasizes the guru's role in guiding disciples towards self realization and liberation.

7. Parrots' forest or aviary.

longest chanting marathon, the largest breathing lesson, and the largest display of bonsai trees. In essence, Sri Ganapathy Sachchidananda Swamiji's life is a harmonious blend of spiritual wisdom, musical artistry, humanitarian service, and environmental stewardship, leaving an indelible mark on countless lives worldwide.

Sri Ganapathy Sachchidananda Swamiji's treatise on Nāda Chikitsa, or sound healing, represents a profound synthesis of ancient Indian musical traditions and contemporary therapeutic practices. This comprehensive work delves into the intricate relationship between sound vibrations and their capacity to influence the human body, mind, and spirit, offering a holistic approach to healing that transcends conventional methodologies.

Background and Genesis of Nāda Chikitsa[8]

The concept of Nāda Chikitsa is deeply rooted in the ancient Indian understanding of sound, or 'Nāda,' as a fundamental force in the universe. Historically, Indian sages recognized the therapeutic potential of specific musical notes and compositions, leading to the development of Raga Chikitsa—a system where particular ragas (melodic frameworks) are employed to address

8. **Nāda Chikitsa** (नादचिकित्सा) is the ancient Indian science of *healing through sound and music.* Rooted in the principles of **Nāda Yoga**, it recognizes that sound vibrations can influence the mind, body, and spirit. **'Nāda'** means sound or vibration, and **'Chikitsa'** means therapy or treatment. Nāda Chikitsa uses specific **ragas, mantras, intonations**, and **frequencies** to harmonize internal energies, calm the mind, and support physical and emotional healing. It is not just about music for relaxation, but a **spiritually oriented, vibrational therapy** believed to balance the **chakras**, purify the **nadis** (energy channels), and attune the individual to higher consciousness. Sri Ganapathy Sachchidananda Swamiji has revitalized and modernized this ancient practice, using **Raga Ragini Vidya** and **Music for Meditation and Healing** concerts to heal and uplift people worldwide.

various physical and psychological ailments. Sri Swamiji, drawing inspiration from this rich heritage, embarked on a mission to revive and modernize these ancient practices, integrating them with contemporary scientific insights to create a robust framework for sound healing. I have dedicated a separate chapter later on, with the fond hope of attempting to explore at least some aspects, including trying to say how Nāda Brahma is an apt title for Sri Swamiji.

Sri Swamiji's Personal Journey and Insights

From a young age, Sri Swamiji exhibited an innate connection to music and its spiritual dimensions. Under the guidance of His mother and mentor, Jayalakshmi Mata, He was initiated into the secrets of music and yoga. His early experiences involved deep observations of nature's sounds and their effects on living beings, leading Him to understand the profound impact of auditory stimuli on the human psyche and physiology. This intuitive grasp was further honed through decades of dedicated practice and research, culminating in His unique approach to Nāda Chikitsa.

Core Principles and Methodologies

At the heart of Sri Swamiji's Nāda Chikitsa is the belief that sound vibrations can directly influence the body's energy centers, or chakras, and the intricate network of nadis (subtle energy channels). Each raga is associated with specific elements, planets, chakras, and even parts of the human body. By meticulously selecting and performing these ragas, Sri Swamiji aims to restore balance and harmony within the individual's energy system. For instance, Raga Charukesi, according to Sri Swamiji, is linked to comprehensive well-being, impacting all chakras and elements, thereby promoting overall health.

Sri Swamiji's therapeutic music sessions are meticulously structured, often incorporating specific hand gestures (mudras) that correspond to the ragas being performed. These mudras are believed to enhance the healing process by facilitating the flow of energy in alignment with the musical vibrations. Participants are guided to adopt these gestures during performances, fostering an immersive and participatory healing experience.

Integration with Other Disciplines

Recognizing the multifaceted nature of healing, Sri Swamiji integrates principles from various disciplines, such as Ayurveda, astrology, gemology, and psychology, into his practice of Nāda Chikitsa. This interdisciplinary approach allows for a more comprehensive understanding of the individual's condition and the formulation of tailored therapeutic interventions. For example, the alignment of specific ragas with astrological signs and planetary influences enables practitioners to address ailments that are believed to have cosmic correlations.

Empirical Evidence and Observations

Over the years, numerous individuals have reported significant improvements in their physical and mental health after participating in Sri Swamiji's music therapy sessions. Conditions ranging from chronic pain and hypertension to depression and anxiety have been alleviated through regular exposure to these healing concerts. Furthermore, preliminary studies have indicated positive behavioral changes among diverse groups, including law enforcement personnel and prison inmates, suggesting the broad applicability of Nāda Chikitsa across various societal contexts.

Contributions to the Global Community

Sri Swamiji's dedication to disseminating the benefits of Nāda Chikitsa has led Him to perform in prestigious venues worldwide, including the Royal Albert Hall in London, the Sydney Opera House, Carnegie Hall in New York, Kennedy Center in New York, Shanmukhananda Hall in Mumbai, and Siri Fort Auditorium in New Delhi, besides the prestigious Rashtrapathi Nilayam in New Delhi. His concerts not only serve as therapeutic sessions but also as platforms for raising awareness about the profound connection between music and healing. Additionally, the establishment of the Nāda Mandapa Auditorium and the Nāda Yoga Research Center in Mysuru stands as a testament to his commitment to advancing the field of music therapy.

Sri Ganapathy Sachchidananda Swamiji's treatise on Nāda Chikitsa offers a transformative perspective on the healing potential of music. By bridging ancient wisdom with modern scientific understanding, He provides a holistic framework that addresses the complexities of human health and well-being. His work not only revitalizes a venerable tradition but also paves the way for future explorations into the therapeutic dimensions of sound, reaffirming the timeless adage that music is indeed a universal language of healing.

CHAPTER 2

How I Came in Contact With Sri Ganapathy Sachchidananda Swamiji

From a nonbeliever to a devoted follower of Pujya Sri Ganapathy Sachchidananda Swamiji in a span of 33 years has been an unbelievable and profoundly enriching spiritual journey for me. I have been a civil servant, having joined one of the prestigious civil services of the Government of India in 1982—the Indian Audit and Accounts Service (IAAS). This service is part of the Comptroller and Auditor General of India (CAG)—the Supreme Audit Institution (SAI) of India. This is equivalent to, say, the National Audit Office (NAO) of the United Kingdom and the Government Accountability Office (GAO) of the United States. I have had postings in different parts of the country—Shimla, Hyderabad, Bengaluru, Kohima in Nagaland, London in the UK, Srinagar in Jammu & Kashmir, Mumbai, Dispur, Assam till I retired from IAAS from CAG, New Delhi as a Director General, at the end of July 2015.

Though I had a posting in Bengaluru from 1986 to 1989 and had passed through Ooty Road and Mysuru umpteen times on official work during the period, I had never visited the Avadhoota Datta Peetham which is located bang on the Mysuru-Ooty highway. It was not until 1991 that through the initiative of my late father-in-law, Sri Ravinutala Venkata Suryanarayana (a retired Income tax officer) that I heard the name and bhajans of Pujya Sri Swamiji for the first time (audio cassettes, those days) when he had brought the cassettes with him to Kohima in Nagaland.

My father-in-law also played a crucial role in bringing me into contact with Pujya Sri Swamiji. He had lost his elder daughter (my wife's sister) in a tragic road accident in Secunderabad in 1990. Sri Swamiji provided tremendous succor and solace to the understandably helpless and distraught family to help them recover from the shock and aftermath of the sad demise of their elder daughter. It was the music cassettes that he had brought along to Kohima in 1991 that appeared very unique to me. The bhajans, especially the tunes and music in albums Nāda Brahma – Celestial Message and Nāda Himalaya, captivated me to no end. Bhajans grew on me slowly, though.

The next stage in my journey was the unexpected shift from the otherwise considered difficult posting in Kohima to London to the overseas audit office in the High Commission of India (HCI) in September 1991. The overseas posting is considered (within Government circles) a sort of recognition of good work done in a difficult place of work. The dilemma was how I would take my wife, who was expecting our second child at the end of 1991, along with me to London, besides taking a young first child of not even 6 years, along too. To top it all, my father-in-law insisted that I come to Mysuru and have the darshan and blessings of Sri Swamiji before proceeding to London. I had other mundane activities to attend to, such as obtaining a diplomatic passport for my family, which was not possible from Kohima or even Guwahati in those days. I had to wind up my establishment in Kohima, arrange for passports, and complete some official formalities with the Ministry of External Affairs and our headquarters, namely CAG in New Delhi. I did not even have a passport, and this was going to be my first travel abroad. Naturally, these were my priorities. I had literally cursed the enthusiasm of my father-in-law, who was blissfully unaware of my predicament, and he had only one thing uppermost in his mind—that somehow, I should have the blessings of Sri Swamiji in Mysuru before leaving for London. There were no direct flights from Dimapur (the nearest airport to Kohima) or even from Guwahati to Bengaluru. I had relegated the possibility of a visit to Mysuru to the very background.

Somehow (in retrospect, due to the invisible hand of Sri Swamiji working), my work in New Delhi proceeded smoothly. Not to displease my well-meaning father-in-law, I managed to travel to Bengaluru, from where we went to Mysuru. The first darshan was not very extraordinary—I must admit—for a nonbeliever. But one thing happened. Sri Swamiji gave a white crystal-like stone (looking like a large sugar lump or crystal) after Ganapathy Homa (Havan)[9] to my son Anirudh, who was suffering from chronic fever and infections over the past 2 years in Kohima. There were no diagnostic facilities, even for what are (now) routine culture tests there. My son put the stone in his mouth, assuming it to be a sugar lump. He took it out after a while when he could not chew or bite it. I was to observe that since that time and later, when we reached London, his chronic fever and infection never surfaced again. In retrospect, I consider it as His first blessing, as my son had been suffering for more than 2 years with an un-diagnosed medical condition.

9. Havan is a scared Vedic ritual involving the offering of ghee, grains, and hearts into a consecrated fire while chanting mantras to invoke divine blessings. It symbolizes purification, devotion, and transformation of material offerings into spiritual energy.

Sri Swamiji blessed us in Mysuru, and my father-in-law was most pleased.

The next significant stage in my journey was when my wife gave birth to our second child—later fondly named Datta Ganesh in November 1991. My wife traveled with me in an advanced stage of pregnancy (the date of travel was the end of October, and the date of delivery was the end of November 1991) without any anxiety or concern—which itself is no mean achievement and happened because of the blessings of Sri Swamiji. Even during the delivery in the labor room, my wife was listening to the bhajans and music of Sri Swamiji. We managed the delivery safely solely because of Sri Swamiji's blessings and nothing else.

Surprisingly, the infant developed a keen attraction to the music since birth. My wife had been listening to the bhajans and music ever since she was pregnant and delivered him while listening to the same. I initially refused to believe that the infant had taken a liking to Sri Swamiji's music. I tested his observations and reactions to the bhajans and music almost every day through September 1992. The video 'Nāda Brahma – the Celestial Message' was his favorite. He would be calm while watching or listening to it and restless till the music or bhajans played, even while traveling in the car. I was left with no alternative but to believe that, indeed, the infant was very positively influenced by and was reacting very visibly to Sri Swamij's music and bhajans. I wanted to test this further.

An opportunity came dramatically. Sri Swamiji was to travel to London in September 1992, which was postponed to the end of November 1992. This coincided with the infant boy's (I call him Datta) first birthday which was on 27 November 1992. I took Datta to the abode (Mr Mukesh Patel's house in Wembley) of Sri Swamiji three days before his birthday. The boy was jumping with joy at the sight of the larger-than-life-size photo of

Sri Swamiji in Mukesh Ji's house. I recorded a video of the first darshan of Sri Swamiji, and boy, how excited Datta was to see Sri Swamiji. This video recording and many others that followed in the three decades thereafter are an everlasting testimony to the special and blessed bond we developed with Sri Swamiji.

We followed this up by attending Sri Swamiji's satsang[10] in the vicinity of Mukesh Ji's house. There, I broached the topic with the organizers, which was my request for Sri Swamiji to visit our house in Champion Hill, Southeast London, on 27 November 1992, Datta's first birthday. Unsurprisingly, I was met with a solid 'NO' from the organizers, who might have planned the programs already, and they could not have accommodated my prayer of a house visit at such short notice. The satsang was about to end when one of the organizers, Mr Jitendra Dave, approached me, asking for my home address and saying that Sri Swamiji would like to visit us exactly on 27 November 1992—the first birthday of Datta. This was a miracle beyond words, and we were all thrilled.

Sri Swamiji came and blessed the boy and us. Some lucky officials and neighbors of the High Commission, London, also had the blessings of Sri Swamiji. This was my first full-fledged interaction with Sri Swamiji. My infant son Datta's deep and demonstrably unbelievable interest and reactions to Sri Swamiji's bhajans and music at such a young age were instrumental in my developing faith in the miraculous powers of His healing music. I had also watched my wife listening to His bhajans and music during the pregnancy and, more particularly, during

10. Satsang is a spiritual gathering where individuals come together in the company of a realized teacher or fellow seekers to engage in truth, wisdom, and inner reflection through discourse, devotional singing, or meditation. The word "satsang" derives from Sanskrit, meaning "association with truth," and is considered a powerful means to uplift the mind and deepen one's spiritual journey.

delivery. The fact that my elder son, Anirudh's, long, troubling bouts of fevers and infection subsided after his 'tasting' the crystal stone in October 1991 also played a significant part in reinforcing my faith in Sri Swamiji.

The second miraculous experience followed, and it was not much later. It was during Sri Swamiji's next visit to London in September 1993. The then President of India, the Late Sri Shankar Dayal Sharma, had visited Avadhoota Datta Peetham in Mysuru even while Sri Swamiji was away from Mysuru in 1993—a great gesture from a spiritually evolved and learned personality. He was visiting London and was staying in the official residence of the High Commissioner of India (HCI) in 9, Kensington Palace in 1993. Sri Swamiji conveyed to me that He was inclined towards visiting the President and wanted me to coordinate the visit, which was at short notice. This was because I was the First Secretary (Director, Audit) at HCI, London.

I considered it to be impossible to organize the visit at such short notice and that too in the official residence of the High Commissioner. The only way to reach the President was through the High Commissioner (Late Dr L.M. Singhvi). The latter said it would not be possible, adding that the First Lady was also indisposed. But, miraculously, within one hour of my approaching the High Commissioner and his dissuading me, his office contacted me, saying that the President had agreed to meet Sri Swamiji in the residence of the High Commissioner. That was the first time Sri Swamiji spoke on the phone with me, asking me to organize the visit. The President received Sri Swamiji with all respect. What struck me was that the President offered a seat that was at a higher level than what he chose to sit on, saying that he could not sit on a chair that was higher than the one on which Sri Swamiji sat. I had the privilege of clicking the first photograph of the President of

India with Sri Swamiji and the High Commissioner. The visit went well. Sri Swamiji was happy and recounted that He had chosen to visit the President because not only was he erudite and scholarly, but he had taken time to visit Avadhoota Datta Peetham even when Sri Swamiji was away. The association of the Late Sri Sharma with Avadhoota Datta Peetham continued further. Sri Swamiji was subsequently invited by the President to give special music for a meditation and healing event in the Rashtrapathi Nilayam to an exclusive audience in 1994.

I would pause here for the moment and continue to my personal journey after discussing two of the most significant contributions and gifts of Sri Swamiji to mankind in the next two chapters. **Nāda Brahma: The Sacred Sound and The Living Resonance of Sri Ganapathy Sachchidananda Swamiji,** followed by **The Healing Power of Music: Insights From Science, Tradition, and Global Experiences**. I follow this up with a review of Bill Osmer's article of December 2006 on Sri Swamiji's music.

I base my discussion in the relevant chapters on primary scriptural and philosophical texts.[11]

---

11. *Avadhoota Gita*, attributed to Bhagawan Dattatreya. A seminal Advaita Vedanta text expressing the nature of a realized Avadhoota. Translation and commentary by Swami Ashokananda (Ramakrishna Mission) and other traditional editions.

• *Srimad Bhagavatam*, Canto 11, Chapters 7–9: Especially the dialogue between Bhagawan Dattatreya and King Yadu, detailing the 24 gurus.

• Tripura Rahasya, especially the section known as Jnana Khanda (the section on supreme knowledge), which contains philosophical teachings attributed to Bhagawan Dattatreya of Sri Ganapathy Sachchidananda Swamiji.

• Jivanmukti Viveka by Swami Vidyaranya—for elaborations on the Avadhoota and Jivanmukta state in classical Vedanta.

The secondary scholarship and interpretative works that I consulted are:

• Swami Sivananda, The *Avadhoota Gita* of Dattatreya (Divine Life Society):

The above apart, I took into account the oral tradition and devotee testimonies, including discourses of Sri Swamiji on *Avadhoota Gita*, Datta Tattva,[12] and Nāda Chikitsa, available in video and audio recordings from the ashram archives and YouTube channel (SGS Videos). I also referred to some personal accounts, experiences, and satsang reflections shared by long-standing devotees and senior disciples, particularly in commemorative volumes and newsletters from Avadhoota Datta Peetham.

Offers both translation and insights into the Avadhoota state from the Advaitic tradition.

• V Rajagopalan, *Dattatreya: The Immortal Guru, Yogin, and Avatara* (MLBD, 2006): A scholarly overview of the mythology, symbolism, and spiritual relevance of Dattatreya and associated lineages.

• RD Ranade, *Mysticism in India: The Poet-Saints of Maharashtra*: Offers contextual parallels with the Nath and Avadhoota schools, especially in relation to Jnana and Bhakti.

I have also extensively referred to the following contemporary context and Sri Swamiji's contributions while writing this book.

• Publications by Avadhoota Datta Peetham, Mysuru.

• Datta Darshanam—A detailed overview of the Dattatreya tradition as interpreted and practiced by Sri Swamiji.

• Sachchidananda: The Life and Mission of Sri Ganapathy Sachchidananda Swamiji—Biographical accounts, teachings, and glimpses into His Avadhoota nature.

• Official website: https://www.dattapeetham.org—includes articles, discourses, interviews, and video/audio content elaborating on Sri Swamiji's views on Dattatreya, Avadhoota, and Nāda Yoga.

• Daniel J. Levitin's *This Is Your Brain on Music* and other music cognition literature for referencing how Sri Swamiji's music aligns with contemporary neurological understandings of sound healing.

12. Datta Tattva encapsulates the philosophical essence of Dattatreya, embodying the unified principles of the Hindu Trinity-Brahma (creation), Vishnu (preservation) and Shiva (destruction)-symbolic ing the cyclical nature of the universe. The concept emphasizes selfles giving (Datta means given), the transcendence of the three qualities and the pursuit of spiritual liberation through the guidance of the eternal guru, Dattatreya.

CHAPTER 3

Nāda Brahma: The Sacred Sound and the Living Resonance of Sri Ganapathy Sachchidananda Swamiji

Abstract

This chapter explores the profound Vedic concept of Nāda Brahma—the idea that the ultimate reality manifests as sound—and presents an in-depth appreciation of how this sacred principle finds living expression in the life and mission of Sri Ganapathy Sachchidananda Swamiji. Drawing from ancient metaphysics, yogic insights, and modern experiential testimony, the chapter examines Sri Swamiji's musical compositions, especially those offered through His music for Meditation and Healing concerts and albums. It investigates the complexity, power, and spiritual efficacy of His sound-based teachings, arguing that Sri Swamiji is not merely a musician or composer but a Nāda Yogi, a realized being who transmits the essence of divine vibration through carefully crafted ragas, mantras, and bhajans. The chapter ultimately affirms that the title Nāda Brahma is not a poetic accolade but an ontological truth in the case of Sri Swamiji—whose presence and music alike reveal the unstruck sound of the cosmos.

The concept of Nāda Brahma lies at the very heart of India's spiritual and metaphysical traditions. It is a sublime assertion that 'Sound is God'—that the ultimate reality, the Absolute, manifests first and foremost as Nāda or primordial sound. According to the Vedic and Tantric cosmologies, before the material universe came into being, there was the formless, ineffable vibration called Anahata Nāda—the unstruck sound—which then differentiated into the sounds of creation. This philosophy finds its expression in the Upanishadic statement, 'Nāda Rūpam Brahma,' meaning Brahman assumes the form of sound. Thus, Nāda Brahma encapsulates the idea that sound is not merely a sensory experience but a spiritual principle, a bridge between the manifest and the unmanifest.

This lofty concept of Nāda Brahma is not a poetic abstraction in the life and mission of Pujya Sri Ganapathy Sachchidananda Swamiji—it is the living pulse of His spiritual work, the very axis around which His teachings and compassionate outreach revolve. To call Him 'Nāda Brahma' is neither hyperbole nor a metaphor—it is a reflection of His embodiment of that eternal sound that uplifts, heals, transforms, and liberates.

Sri Swamiji's musical compositions are not created in the usual artistic sense; they are downloads from silence, intuitive flows from a plane far deeper than intellect or emotion. His music carries the vibratory essence of mantras, ragas, and sacred geometry, forming a seamless synthesis of classical Indian musicality with yogic insight and meditative power. Each of His ragas is more than a scale or tune—it is an expression of a specific bhava (emotion), a healing frequency, a spiritual key to unlock subtle dimensions of consciousness.

In public concerts and private recordings, Sri Swamiji doesn't merely perform—He transmits. His role is not that of a performer or even a composer but of a Nāda Yogi, one who has mastered the science of sound as a spiritual sadhana. His

'Music for Meditation and Healing' series and international concerts such as 'Raga Sagara,' 'Nāda Sangama,' and 'Nāda Chikitsa,' are not entertainment programs but collective sadhana[13]—initiations through sound. Thousands have reported inner shifts, emotional release, health benefits, and mystical experiences through His music, testifying to the power of Nāda when wielded by a realized master.

Equally profound is the silence that follows His music. The stillness after a bhajan or raga played by Sri Swamiji is not emptiness—it is the presence of pure consciousness, invoked by the wave of Nāda and lingering long after the last note has faded. This is perhaps the most authentic test of Nāda Brahma: does the music leave one in contact with Brahman, the Self? In Sri Swamiji's case, the answer is unequivocally yes.

Furthermore, His entire persona is steeped in sound—from the spontaneous bhajans (more than 3,000 in different languages) He sings, often composed in divine ecstasy, to the powerful mantras He bestows for protection and healing, to the unique ragas He has composed and documented for therapeutic use. He has also inspired and trained hundreds to become vehicles of divine sound, ensuring that the tradition of Nāda Yoga continues for future generations.

It is thus not for nothing that Sri Ganapathy Sachchidananda Swamiji is universally recognized as 'Nāda Brahma.' It is not only apt—it is a recognition of His divine identity as the Sound Incarnate, a being who does not merely teach through words but through vibration itself. His life is a testament to the power of sacred sound as both a means and an end in the spiritual

13. Sadhana is a disciplined spiritual practice undertaken with dedication to attain inner growth, self-realization, or union with the Divine. It can include meditation, mantra chanting, yoga, prayer, or service, performed regularly with sincerity and focus.

journey. He has brought the Vedic vision of Nāda Brahma down from metaphysical heights into the palpable realm of lived experience, making the music of the soul audible once again to a world in desperate need of inner harmony.

The concept of Nāda Brahma stands as one of the most elevated formulations in the Indian spiritual tradition—a recognition that the universe, at its most essential level, is vibration and that this vibration is sacred. While this insight has guided sages, yogis, and mystics for millennia, it finds a unique, tangible, and transformative expression in the divine life and mission of Sri Ganapathy Sachchidananda Swamiji. His music, unlike that of even the greatest classical maestros, does not seek aesthetic achievement alone; it seeks inner alignment, emotional healing, and spiritual awakening. His compositions are structured with the precision of a rishi and performed with the surrender of a saint, acting not merely as sounds but as sacred transmissions of chaitanya—pure consciousness. The concepts of naḍīs and Nāda Chikitsa are thus deeply rooted in both scriptural authority and contemporary exploration, blending ancient yogic wisdom with modern insights from science and musicology.

From the traditional and scriptural standpoint, the yogic understanding of naḍīs—the subtle energy channels that carry praṇa or life force—finds prominent mention in several authoritative texts of Hatha Yoga[14] and Tantra. The Hatha Yoga

14. Hatha Yoga is a branch of yoga that focuses on physical postures (asanas), breathing techniques (pranayama), and cleansing practices (kriyas) to prepare the body and mind for higher states of meditation. 'Ha' means sun, and 'Tha' means moon—symbolizing the union of opposing energies. It aims to purify and balance the body, control prana (life force), and ultimately lead to spiritual awakening.

Tantra is a broader spiritual science that encompasses rituals, mantras, meditative practices, and esoteric techniques to expand consciousness and

Pradīpika, a seminal 15th-century yogic manual, offers one of the clearest early references to naḍīs. In Chapter 2, Verse 4, it states that there are 72,000 naḍīs in the human body, forming a subtle network through which energy flows. Verses 5 and 6 of the same chapter describe the three[15] most important naḍīs: Ida, Piṅgala, and Suṣumna, each governing distinct aspects of physical, mental, and spiritual experience. The Shiva Saṁhita,[16] another influential text, offers detailed anatomical and spiritual insights into these channels, emphasizing the purification of suṣumna for the awakening of higher consciousness. Similarly, the Gheraṇḍa Saṁhita[17] discusses naḍī shuddhi (cleansing of

---

attain liberation. It views the body and universe as interconnected and divine and emphasizes the awakening of kundalinī shakti (spiritual energy). Contrary to popular misconception, true Tantra is highly disciplined, sacred, and rooted in deep yogic and philosophical principles.

15. Ida Nadi is the lunar energy channel in yoga, associated with the left side of the body and the mind, promoting calmness and introspection. Pingala Nadi is the solar energy channel linked to the right side of the body and the vital force, encouraging activity and dynamism. Sushumna Nadi is the central channel that runs along the spine, through which spiritual energy (Kundalini) ascends when Ida and Piṅgala are balanced, leading to higher states of consciousness.

16. The Shiva Samhita is a classic Sanskrit text on Hatha Yoga, attributed to Lord Shiva, that offers detailed instructions on asanas (postures), mudras (gestures), pranayama (breath control), and the awakening of kundalini. It presents a non-dualistic (Advaita) philosophy, asserting that the individual self is identical to the supreme Self (Shiva), and that liberation comes through inner realization. Unlike some other yogic texts, it also acknowledges the possibility of householders attaining enlightenment, making it accessible to both renunciants and lay practitioners.

17. The Gheraṇḍa Samhita is a classical 17th-century Sanskrit text on Hatha Yoga, presented as a dialogue between the sage Gheraṇḍa and his disciple Chanda. It outlines a comprehensive seven-step path (sapta sadhana) to perfection, including purification (shatkarma), postures (asana), gestures (mudra), breath control (pranayama), sensory withdrawal (pratyahara), meditation (dhyana), and absorption (samadhi). Emphasizing discipline and gradual progress, the text combines physical practices with spiritual goals, aiming to transform the body into a fit vessel for self-realization.

naḍīs) as a foundational practice essential for progress in yogic disciplines.

Parallel to the physiology of naḍīs is the spiritual science of sound, or nāda. The Nāda Bindu Upaniṣad,[18] associated with the Rig Veda[19] and Sama Veda[20] traditions, introduces the idea that sound is not merely an external phenomenon but a subtle inner vibration that can be accessed through deep meditation. Verse 39 of this Upaniṣad affirms that when the mind is absorbed in the unstruck sound (anahata nāda), it merges with Brahman, the ultimate reality. This concept is closely linked to Nāda Yoga, the spiritual path of inner sound. The teachings of Bhagawan

18. The Nāda Bindu Upanishad is a minor Upanishad of the Rigveda or Atharvaveda that explores the yogic path of sound (Nāda Yoga) as a means to attain liberation. It teaches that by meditating on the inner sound (Nāda)—culminating in the subtle, formless vibration—the yogi transcends the mind and realizes the Self (Atman). The text emphasizes that sound is both the means and the manifestation of Brahman, and through deep concentration on the sound 'Om,' the seeker merges into supreme consciousness.

19. The Rig Veda is the oldest and most revered of the four Vedas, composed in Vedic Sanskrit around 1500 BCE, and consists of over 1,000 hymns (suktas) dedicated to various deities like Agni, Indra, and Varuna. It is a profound collection of cosmic poetry, ritual chants, and philosophical insights, reflecting the spiritual and cultural life of early Vedic society. Beyond its liturgical use, the Rig Veda also contains deep metaphysical reflections on creation, existence, and the nature of the divine.

20. The Sama Veda is the Veda of melody and chants, consisting mostly of hymns taken from the Rig Veda but arranged specifically for musical and ritualistic singing. It forms the foundation of Indian classical music and emphasizes the power of sound and vibration in spiritual practice. Used by priests during Vedic sacrifices, the Sama Veda transforms sacred words into divine music, aiming to elevate consciousness and invoke harmony with the cosmos.

Dattatreya,[21] especially through the *Avadhūta Gīta,*[22] also refer to subtle inner-auditory experiences that align with the philosophy of nāda anusandhana—the meditative pursuit of inner sound vibrations. Furthermore, the Sama Veda, the Veda of music and chants, and its subtext, the Gandharva Veda, provide the foundation for Indian classical music. The Gandharva Veda, in particular, articulates the power of musical modes (ragas) to influence consciousness, emotions, and health, thereby directly supporting the principles behind Nāda Chikitsa.

In more recent times, these ancient insights have been brought into contemporary relevance through the pioneering work of spiritual masters such as Sri Ganapathy Sachchidananda Swamiji. In His discourses and publications, such as Music for Meditation and Healing, Sri Swamiji elucidates the science and spiritual depth of Nāda Chikitsa. According to Sri Swamiji, specific ragas resonate with particular chakras or cakras[23] and

21. Dattatreya is a revered deity in Hinduism, considered the embodiment of the Divine Trinity—Brahma (the creator), Vishnu (the preserver), and Shiva (the destroyer)—in a single form. He is seen as the Adi Guru (first teacher) of the Avadhoota tradition and is a symbol of detachment, wisdom, and spiritual liberation. Often depicted with three heads and six hands, Dattatreya is associated with yogic knowledge, mysticism, and universal compassion. His teachings emphasize learning from nature and the world itself as a spiritual guide.

22. The Avadhūta Gīta is a profound Advaita Vedanta scripture attributed to Bhagawan Dattatreya, expressing the spontaneous wisdom of an enlightened being beyond all dualities. It declares the self as pure, formless, infinite consciousness, untouched by body, mind, or world, and free from bondage or liberation. With radical non-duality at its core, the text dismisses ritual, religion, and conventional knowledge, affirming that 'I am neither the doer nor the enjoyer—I am pure awareness alone.'

23. In yoga, the main chakras are energy centers aligned along the Sushumna Nadi, the central channel running through the spine, and they play a vital role in the flow and balance of pranic energy (life force). There are seven principal chakras: Muladhara (Root Chakra) – Located at the base of the spine, it anchors physical existence and survival instincts; it's the starting point of the Sushumna Nadi and the dormant Kundalini energy. Svadhishthana (Sacral Chakra)

energy pathways, enabling deep healing and transformation when performed with devotion and precision. His healing concerts have drawn global attention, not merely for their musical richness but for their demonstrable therapeutic effects. Anecdotal evidence, as well as informal clinical observations, suggest improvements in emotional well-being, mental clarity, and even physiological parameters in listeners.

Scientific inquiry into the efficacy of music therapy more broadly provides indirect support for Sri Swamiji's approach. Although no formal, published studies have yet evaluated Sri Swamiji's concerts specifically, AIIMS[24] or NIMHANS[25] have examined the broader domain of music therapy as a subject of controlled clinical research. A study conducted at AIIMS, New Delhi, titled 'Effect of Music on Pain Intensity and Physiological

– Situated below the navel, it governs creativity, emotions, and sensuality, influencing the flow of energy between lower and higher centers. Manipura (Solar Plexus Chakra) – Found above the navel, it regulates willpower, confidence, and transformation, energizing the body through pranic fire. Anahata (Heart Chakra) – At the center of the chest, it bridges the lower and upper chakras and balances love, compassion, and emotional healing. Vishuddha (Throat Chakra) – Located at the throat, it governs communication, truth, and purification, influencing the vibrational aspect of energy. Ajna (Third Eye Chakra) – Between the eyebrows, it is the seat of intuition and insight, where Ida and Pingala Nadis converge with Sushumna, aiding in inner vision and clarity. Sahasrara (Crown Chakra) – At the top of the head, it represents pure consciousness and spiritual enlightenment, where the awakened Kundalini merges with universal energy. These chakras regulate the flow of prana through the nadis, and their awakening through sadhana—including pranayama, meditation, and mantra—leads to spiritual evolution and self-realization.

24. All India Institute of Medical Sciences, New Delhi.

25. NIMHANS stands for National Institute of Mental Health and Neurosciences. It is a premier medical institution located in Bengaluru, India, specializing in mental health, neurosciences, and psychiatric education, research, and care. Established in 1974, NIMHANS operates under the Ministry of Health and Family Welfare and is recognized as an Institute of National Importance.

Parameters among Post-Operative Cardiac Patients,'[26] demonstrated that patients who listened to calming music after surgery experienced statistically significant reductions in pain and improvements in heart rate and blood pressure compared to those who received routine care alone. Though the study did not focus on Nāda Chikitsa or raga-based music, its findings underscore the validity of sound as a therapeutic modality.

Complementing these spiritual and scientific sources are contributions from scholars and thinkers who explore the interface between sound, neuroscience, and culture. Daniel J. Levitin's bestselling work 'This Is Your Brain on Music' presents empirical evidence (I discuss further in Chapter 4) on how music shapes brain chemistry, emotion, and memory. While Levitin writes from a Western scientific perspective, his findings lend credence to the Indian view that music can be harnessed for deep psychological and physiological impact. Dr T.M. Krishna, in his cultural and philosophical study *A Southern Music: The Karnatik Story*,[27] discusses the metaphysical and emotional power of ragas, highlighting how aesthetic experience (rasa) becomes a gateway to inner transformation. Alain Daniélou, the French musicologist and Indologist, explores similar territory in his book 'Music and the Power of Sound,'[28] where he draws upon Indian metaphysical thought to

26. www.reaearchgate.net; www.academia.edu-A study to evaluate the effect of music on pain intensity and physiological parameters among post-operative cardiac patients in AIIMS, New Delhi; International Journal of Science and Research (IISR)-ISSN(online): 2319-7064- February 2015.

27. Krishna, T.M., *The Karnatik Story: A Journey Through the South Indian Music Tradition*. HarperCollins India, 2020.

28. www.alaindanielou.org; the book explores the development of musical scales and tuning systems from their origins in China and India through their fusion in Ancient Greece, to the evolution of western modal and polyphonic traditions. He emphasizes how simple harmonic ratios in music can directly influence higher

argue that sound is not only a sensory experience but a spiritual force with the potential to reorder consciousness and matter.

Together, these traditional texts, contemporary experiments, and spiritual interpretations form a rich and coherent tapestry that supports the interlinked concepts of naḍīs and Nāda Chikitsa. They affirm that the human being is not merely a physical organism but a finely tuned instrument whose strings—when played through sacred sound—can harmonize the inner and outer cosmos.

In every raga rendered, every bhajan sung, and every silent pause between notes, Sri Swamiji reveals the presence of Nāda as Brahman. For those attuned to it, His music is not performance—it is darshana. It is an encounter with the divine not through form, word, or doctrine but through vibration itself. Thus, calling Him Nāda Brahma is not only fitting—it is inevitable. It is the acknowledgment that through His life, His voice, and His music, Sri Swamiji has brought the silence of the Absolute into audible form. He has made the cosmic sound not only accessible but healing, not only sacred but immediate. In a world craving harmony, Sri Swamiji's music reminds us that the path to God may well begin with listening—not just with the ears, but with the soul.

---

consciousness, which allows modern musicians to transcend the limitations of overly rationalistic music by reconnecting with its metaphysical roots.

CHAPTER 4

The Healing Power of Music: Insights from Science, Tradition, and Global Experiences

Abstract

Music has long been recognized as a source of solace, spiritual elevation, and physical healing across cultures and civilizations. From the ancient traditions of Nāda Yoga in India to contemporary neuroscience-backed music therapy, the therapeutic power of sound continues to influence and transform human well-being. This comprehensive exploration delves into various dimensions of music as a healing force, drawing insights from Daniel J. Levitin's Music as Medicine, the pioneering work of Sri Ganapathy Sachchidananda Swamiji on Nāda Chikitsa, and global research on music therapy. By integrating perspectives from neuroscience, traditional Indian healing practices, and modern clinical applications, this chapter underscores the role of music as a potent tool for enhancing mental, physical, and emotional health.

The Neuroscience of Music Therapy: Daniel J. Levitin's[29] Perspective

Daniel J. Levitin, an acclaimed neuroscientist and musician, provides a compelling scientific foundation for understanding the healing power of music in his book *Music as Medicine*. His work explores how music influences multiple regions of the brain, including those responsible for perception, emotion, memory, and motor functions. Levitin highlights the role of neurotransmitters such as serotonin and dopamine, which are essential for mood regulation and motivation, and shows how engaging with music can increase their levels, thereby improving mental well-being. Conversely, music has been shown to reduce cortisol levels, diminishing stress and anxiety.

Levitin underscores the importance of personalized music therapy, demonstrating that individual preferences in musical selections significantly affect therapeutic outcomes. A striking example from his book is the case of singer-songwriter Joni Mitchell, who, following a severe stroke, regained speech and mobility through a customized music therapy program incorporating her favorite songs. His research also delves into rhythmic auditory stimulation, which has been particularly effective for individuals with movement disorders such as Parkinson's disease. Structured rhythms in music can act as external cues, facilitating improved gait and coordination.

---

29. Daniel J. Levitin's book, *I Heard There Was a Secret Chord: Music as Medicine*, explores the profound connections between music and healing. Published on August 27, 2024, by W.W. Norton & Company, this work delves into how music can serve as a potent therapeutic tool, aiding in the treatment of various ailments such as neurodegenerative diseases, cognitive injuries, depression, and pain. In the United Kingdom and international markets, the book is titled *Music as Medicine: How We Can Harness Its Therapeutic Power*.

Moreover, Levitin examines how active engagement with music, such as playing an instrument or singing, enhances neuroplasticity. This process fosters the creation of new neural pathways, potentially delaying the onset of dementia-related symptoms. By presenting scientific evidence and real-life case studies, *Music as Medicine* makes a compelling argument for integrating music-based interventions into mainstream medical and psychological practices.

Sri Ganapathy Sachchidananda Swamiji's Contributions to Healing Through Music

Sri Ganapathy Sachchidananda Swamiji, has significantly expanded the discourse on music therapy by integrating ancient Indian musical traditions with holistic healing practices. His teachings emphasize the therapeutic properties of specific musical scales, known as ragas, which influence physical, mental, and spiritual well-being. Central to His philosophy is Raga Ragini Vidya, which explores the intricate relationship between musical notes and human emotions.

Sri Swamiji's approach is deeply rooted in Nāda Yoga,[30] an ancient discipline that posits sound vibrations as a fundamental force influencing the body's energy centers, or chakras. By aligning particular ragas with specific emotional states, His compositions aim to induce desired psychological and physiological responses. His concerts, collectively known as Raga Sagara (Ocean of Ragas), have been performed at globally

30. Nāda Yoga is the ancient yogic science of union through sound. It teaches that sound (nāda)—both external and internal—is a powerful medium to connect the individual self (jīvatman) with the universal consciousness (paramatman). It involves deep listening, chanting of mantras, and meditative focus on subtle inner sounds (known as anahata nāda). Nāda Yoga sees the entire universe as vibration, and through disciplined practice, it helps transcend the mind, balance energy, and attain spiritual awakening.

renowned venues such as the Royal Albert Hall in London, the Sydney Opera House, and the Lincoln Center and Carnegie Hall in New York. These performances have been widely acclaimed for their ability to promote meditation, relaxation, and healing.

Sri Swamiji's therapeutic methodology is comprehensive, integrating various elements such as self-composed lyrics containing resonant seed syllables like 'Om,'[31] astrological calculations, the healing energy of crystals and gems, specific bonsai trees, and bird sounds associated with each raga. These elements collectively contribute to the precise selection of musical frequencies tailored to individual needs in both live therapy sessions and studio recordings.

The practical efficacy of Sri Swamiji's music therapy has been observed in diverse settings, including hospitals, educational institutions, and correctional facilities. Patients suffering from psychosomatic ailments, chronic conditions, and terminal illnesses have reported significant relief after engaging with His music. Notably, His compositions have been used to alleviate stress among police personnel and inmates, demonstrating the broad applicability of his therapeutic music. His contributions to Nāda Chikitsa were recognized by Sri Krishnadevaraya University (2013), World Classical Tamil University, London(2016), and Dr Gangubai Hanagal Music & Performing Arts University, Karnataka (2023) when they awarded Pujya Sri Swamiji with doctorates and Honoris Causa – Doctor of Letters.

---

31. In Nāda Yoga, 'Om' is the primordial sound (Anahata Nāda) from which all creation arises—the subtle vibration that underlies the entire cosmos. Chanting or meditating on Om attunes the practitioner to this inner, unstruck sound, helping dissolve the ego and awaken higher states of consciousness. It serves as both the path and the destination, leading the seeker from outer sound to inner silence and union with the Divine.

Nāda Chikitsa: Healing Through Sound

Sri Ganapathy Sachchidananda Swamiji has extensively propagated Nāda Chikitsa, or healing through music, in His addresses at various global music events. His philosophy is based on the understanding that Nāda (sound) is a cosmic force with the intrinsic ability to influence the human mind, body, and spirit. He asserts that specific musical notes and ragas can restore balance and promote healing by resonating with the body's energy centers. Sri Swamiji's music is multi-faceted. In concerts, Sri Swamiji plays His own compositions on the synthesizer and is accompanied by musicians (melody and rhythm sections separately seated) playing classical Indian instruments. Healing and meditation music is, in essence, music therapy and an essential part of Sri Swamiji's mission to bring peace to the world. His music is very unique, as He follows the ancient concept of using pure sounds—Nāda—and ancient medicinal melodies. Sri Swamiji's music is also devotional and is used as a vehicle for spiritual energy transmission.

In His public discourses, Sri Swamiji emphasizes how listening to carefully selected ragas can alleviate stress, enhance mental clarity, and elevate spiritual consciousness. His concerts are meticulously structured to facilitate meditation and healing, serving not just as artistic expressions but as profound therapeutic experiences. By immersing listeners in specific ragas, He seeks to create an environment conducive to self-healing and spiritual awakening. Through His global initiatives, Sri Swamiji continues to advocate for integrating the healing potential of music into daily life, encouraging individuals to harness its power for holistic health and well-being.

Raga Ragini Nāda Yoga:[32] A Treatise on the Healing Power of Music

Sri Swamiji's book, *Raga Ragini Nāda Yoga*, is a seminal contribution to the study of music therapy. It elucidates the therapeutic properties of specific ragas and their correlation with human physiology and emotional states. According to this treatise, different ragas are linked to various chakras and elements within the human body, influencing specific physiological functions and promoting healing.

One of the core principles of Raga Ragini Vidya is the transformative power of sound vibrations. Sri Swamiji explains that the human body contains 72,000 metaphysical energy channels (nadis), each vibrating at a specific frequency. Disruptions in these vibrations can lead to illness, but by applying appropriate ragas, one can restore harmony and well-being. While deeply rooted in traditional Indian spiritual and medicinal practices, the book suggests that further empirical validation through contemporary scientific methodologies could enhance the credibility of these therapeutic claims.

In essence, Raga Ragini Vidya serves as a bridge between ancient musical wisdom and holistic health practices. Sri Swamiji's insights encourage practitioners and researchers alike to explore the healing potentials of music, fostering a synthesis of spirituality, art, and medicine.

32. Raga Ragiṇī Vidya is the sacred science of understanding the spiritual and healing power of melodic frameworks (ragas and ragiṇīs) in Indian classical music. Raga refers to a melodic mode, each with its own emotional essence (rasa), time of performance, and healing effect. Ragiṇī is the feminine counterpart or variation of a raga. This vidya (knowledge) is not merely musical—it is deeply symbolic, linking sound with cosmic energy, emotions, and consciousness. Practiced by saints, yogis, and mystics, Raga Ragiṇī Vidya is central to Nāda Chikitsa (sound therapy) and devotional music, as revived and taught by Sri Ganapathy Sachchidananda Swamiji.

International Perspectives on the Healing Power of Music

Across the globe, music therapy has been increasingly recognized as a valuable non-pharmacological intervention for various health conditions. Research studies have demonstrated that music can significantly improve cognitive functions, particularly in individuals with neurodegenerative disorders. For instance, a Yale University study[33] explored the effects of Latin dance music on seniors, showing improvements in balance, attention, cognitive flexibility, and processing speed. Similarly, personalized music therapy has been found effective in pain management, with research from McGill University[34] indicating that music aligned with an individual's natural tempo can reduce pain perception.

Music's ability to evoke autobiographical memories has also been harnessed in therapeutic settings, particularly for individuals with Alzheimer's disease. Furthermore, clinical studies have revealed that post-operative patients who listen to music experience reduced pain, anxiety, and heart rates, leading to improved recovery outcomes. This growing body of research

33. A Yale University study is exploring how Latin dance can benefit seniors' physical and cognitive health. Led by Assistant Professor Dr Luke Kun Liu and dance therapeutic instructor Freddy Ramirez, the program involves hour-long Latin dance sessions twice a week at Hartford's South End Wellness Senior Center. Early findings indicate improvements in participants' grip strength, balance, attention, cognitive flexibility, processing speed, and mood. While not a cure for Alzheimer's disease, the researchers hope this approach can serve as an alternative means to enhance overall cognitive and physical well-being in seniors.

34. The McGill University study on music and pain management was published on February 3, 2025. The research suggests that music aligned with an individual's natural rhythm significantly reduces pain perception, indicating that personalizing music tempo to match one's internal rhythm can enhance its analgesic effects. https://www.mcgill.ca/newsroom/channels/news/when-using-music-alleviate-pain-tempo-matters-362884

underscores the increasing acceptance of music therapy as a vital component of modern healthcare.

The universal recognition of music's healing power, spanning neuroscientific research, traditional Indian practices, and global clinical studies, affirms its profound impact on human health and well-being. Whether through the scientific lens of Daniel J. Levitin, the spiritual wisdom of Sri Ganapathy Sachchidananda Swamiji, or international medical research, music emerges as a versatile and effective therapeutic tool. As society continues to explore holistic approaches to healing, the integration of music therapy into mainstream healthcare holds immense promise, offering a natural, accessible, and deeply enriching means to enhance physical, mental, and emotional well-being.

As mentioned earlier, Daniel J. Levitin's book, *Music as Medicine*, delves into the profound relationship between music and healing, exploring how musical interventions can serve as potent therapeutic tools. Historically, various cultures have harnessed the power of music to alleviate suffering, promote healing, and soothe the mind. Levitin, both a neuroscientist and an accomplished musician, investigates contemporary scientific findings to demonstrate how music can aid in treating a spectrum of ailments, including neurodegenerative diseases like Parkinson's[35] and Alzheimer's,[36] cognitive impairments, depression, and chronic pain.

35. Parkinson's disease is a progressive neurological disorder that primarily affects movement, causing symptoms such as tremors, stiffness, and balance difficulties. These result from the degeneration of dopamine-producing neurons in the brain's substantial Nigar region.

36. Alzheimer's is a progressive neuro degenerative disorder that gradually destroys memory and cognitive abilities, eventually impairing the ability to carry out simple tasks. It is characterized by the accumulation of amyloid plaques and neurofibrillary tangles in the brain, leading to the death of nerve cells and brain atrophy.

Central to Levitin's exploration is the understanding that music influences numerous brain regions responsible for perception, emotion, memory, and motor functions. He elucidates that engaging with music can lead to increased levels of neurotransmitters such as serotonin and dopamine, which are vital for mood regulation and motivation. Conversely, music can reduce cortisol levels, thereby diminishing stress. These neurochemical changes underpin music's capacity to serve as a therapeutic modality.

Levitin underscores the significance of personalized music therapy, emphasizing that individual preferences play a crucial role in therapeutic outcomes. He presents compelling case studies, such as the recovery journey of singer-songwriter Joni Mitchell (mentioned earlier) following a severe stroke. Mitchell's tailored music therapy program, which incorporated her favorite songs, was instrumental in her rehabilitation, aiding in the restoration of her speech and mobility.

The book also examines the application of rhythmic auditory stimulation in improving motor functions for patients with movement disorders. For instance, individuals with Parkinson's disease often experience enhanced gait and coordination when engaging with rhythmically structured music, which can serve as an external cue to facilitate movement.

Levitin further explores how active participation in music, such as playing an instrument or singing, can bolster cognitive functions and potentially delay the onset of dementia-related symptoms. This engagement fosters the creation of new neural pathways, enhancing neuroplasticity and cognitive resilience.

In conclusion, *Music as Medicine* presents a compelling narrative on the therapeutic potential of music, supported by scientific research and enriched with real-life examples. Levitin advocates for the integration of music-based interventions into conventional medical practices, proposing that music serves not only as a source of entertainment but also as a valuable component in holistic healing and well-being.

Let me now come to Sri Ganapathy Sachchidananda Swamiji, who has significantly contributed to the realm of music therapy through His innovative integration of traditional Indian music and healing practices. His work emphasizes the therapeutic potential of specific musical scales, known as ragas, in promoting physical, mental, and spiritual well-being.

Central to Sri Swamiji's approach is the concept of 'Raga Ragini Vidya,' which explores the intricate relationship between musical notes and human emotions. By aligning particular ragas with specific emotional states, His compositions aim to induce desired psychological and physiological responses in listeners. This method is deeply rooted in the ancient Indian tradition of Nāda Yoga, which posits that sound vibrations can influence the body's energy centers or chakras, thereby facilitating healing and spiritual growth.

Sri Swamiji's musical journey is marked by His mastery of the synthesizer, affectionately termed the 'Modern Veena.' Since 1987, He has redefined music concerts[37] by focusing on meditation and healing, performing globally, as mentioned earlier, in prestigious venues such as the Royal Albert Hall in London, the Sydney Opera House, and the Carnegie Hall in New York. These concerts, often titled 'Raga Sagara' or 'Ocean of Ragas,' have attracted diverse audiences, including both novices and scholars and have been lauded for their calming and restorative effects.

In His therapeutic sessions, Sri Swamiji employs a holistic approach that combines various disciplines. He integrates

37. Sri Swamiji has blessed humanity with more than 350 Music for Meditation and Healing events across famous venues in all corners of the world.

Indian ragas based on their aesthetic appeal, self-composed lyrics containing resonant seed syllables like 'Om,' astrological calculations, the healing energy of crystals and gems, relevant bonsai trees, and specific bird sounds associated with each raga. This multifaceted methodology is designed to select appropriate music frequencies tailored to individual needs during live therapy sessions and studio recordings.

The efficacy of Sri Swamiji's music therapy has been observed across various settings, including hospitals, educational institutions, and correctional facilities. Individuals suffering from psychosomatic ailments, chronic conditions, and terminal illnesses have reported significant relief and improved quality of life after engaging with his music. Furthermore, his compositions have been utilized to reduce stress among police personnel and inmates, highlighting the broad applicability of his therapeutic music.

In recognition of His contributions to music and healing, Sri Swamiji has been honored with several accolades. Notably, in 2013, Sri Krishnadevaraya University conferred upon him an honorary doctorate for His treatise *Raga Ragini Nāda Yoga*, underscoring His impact on the world of music therapy. On 23 May 2016, World Classical Tamil University, London bestowed upon Sri Swamiji the Honoris Causa – Doctor of Letters. On 31 Oct 2023, Karnataka State Dr Gangubai Hanagal Music and Performing Arts University, Karnataka, bestowed upon Sri Swamiji the Honorary Doctorate in Music. Sri Ganapathy Sachchidananda Swamiji's integration of traditional Indian musical elements with holistic healing practices has pioneered a unique form of music therapy. His work continues to inspire and benefit individuals worldwide, fostering a deeper appreciation for the therapeutic potential of music. He has extensively propagated the concept of 'Nāda Chikitsa,' or healing through music. Through His global music events, He has elucidated the profound connection between sound vibrations and holistic well-being, integrating ancient wisdom with contemporary therapeutic practices.

Sri Swamiji's philosophy is the belief that 'Nāda' (sound) serves as a fundamental force in the universe, possessing the intrinsic ability to influence the mind, body, and spirit. He posits that specific musical notes and ragas (melodic frameworks in Indian classical music) can resonate with the body's energy centers or chakras, thereby restoring balance and promoting healing. This perspective aligns with the ancient Indian tradition of 'Nāda Yoga,' which emphasizes the union of the individual consciousness with the universal through the medium of sound.

In His addresses during various music events worldwide, Sri Swamiji has highlighted the therapeutic potential of music in alleviating stress, anxiety, and other psychosomatic ailments. He asserts that listening to carefully selected ragas can induce relaxation, enhance mental clarity, and elevate spiritual consciousness. By attuning oneself to these healing vibrations, individuals can experience a harmonious state of being, leading to improved health and inner peace.

Sri Swamiji's concerts, titled 'Raga Sagara' (Ocean of Ragas), are meticulously designed to facilitate meditation and healing. These performances are not merely artistic expressions but are also considered therapeutic sessions aimed at transforming the audience's inner landscape. By immersing listeners in specific ragas, He endeavors to create an environment conducive to self-healing and spiritual awakening. Through His global initiatives, Sri Swamiji continues to inspire individuals to explore the healing potential of music, advocating for its integration into daily life as a means to achieve holistic health and spiritual fulfillment.

At its core, 'Raga Ragini Vidya' elucidates the concept that specific musical scales, or ragas, possess inherent therapeutic properties capable of influencing the physical and mental states of individuals. Drawing from ancient scriptures and personal experiences, Sri Swamiji articulates how different ragas correspond to various energy centers (chakras) and elements within the human body. For instance, certain ragas are believed to resonate with particular chakras, thereby promoting healing and balance in associated bodily functions.

Critically, while 'Raga Ragini Vidya' offers profound insights into the intersection of music and healing, it operates predominantly within the paradigms of traditional Indian spiritual and medicinal practices. The therapeutic claims associated with specific ragas, though rooted in centuries-old traditions, may benefit from empirical validation through contemporary scientific methodologies. Integrating modern research with traditional knowledge could enhance the credibility and acceptance of these practices in broader therapeutic contexts. 'Raga Ragini Vidya' serves as a valuable bridge connecting ancient musical wisdom with holistic health practices. Sri Swamiji's exposition invites readers and practitioners to explore the healing potential of music, encouraging a harmonious blend of art, spirituality, and well-being.

Sri Swamiji's Music for Meditation and Healing concerts, held across some of the world's most iconic and spiritually resonant venues, represent a unique confluence of ancient Indian spiritual tradition, raga-based music, and cutting-edge therapeutic intent. These events are not mere musical performances—they are sacred transmissions, meticulously crafted for the elevation of human consciousness and the subtle healing of body, mind, and spirit. What distinguishes Swamiji's concerts is not only the divine nature of the compositions but also the purpose and energy they embody: each note is infused with praṇa (life force), each raga is chosen for its impact on the subtle body, and each concert hall becomes, for those hours, a temple of healing through sound.

One of the most iconic manifestations of this vision unfolded at the Royal Albert Hall in London on July 15, 2018. This concert marked a milestone in the global recognition of Sri Swamiji's Nāda Chikitsa movement. The Royal Albert Hall, known for hosting the world's finest musical talents, reverberated with Sri Swamiji's celestial compositions, structured in specific ragas chosen to correspond with energy centers within the human body. The grandeur of the setting only amplified the spiritual subtlety of the experience. Thousands of seekers, spiritual aspirants, and curious attendees from different faiths and nationalities gathered to witness what many described as a concert of divine vibrations. The event was a testament to the universal appeal of Sri Swamiji's music, transcending cultural and linguistic boundaries to speak directly to the soul.

Earlier, on April 6, 2015, a historic event took place at the Sydney Opera House, Australia's most iconic cultural landmark. Sri Swamiji led what was recognized by Guinness World Records as the largest music therapy session in the world. With over 1,800 participants, the Opera House was transformed into a sanctuary of meditative sound. Sri Swamiji's compositions, rooted in traditional raga structures yet rendered through modern instrumentation, resonated across the vaulted interiors of the hall, touching every heart present. It was not just a display of musical mastery but a demonstration of music's power to harmonize collective consciousness. Participants reported profound experiences ranging from inner peace to emotional catharsis, validating the premise that Sri Swamiji's music functions as vibrational medicine.

Sri Swamiji's concerts at Shanmukhananda Hall in Mumbai, one of India's premier venues for classical music and devotional gatherings, were particularly significant. The Mumbai audience, steeped in the traditions of Carnatic and Hindustani music,[38] could appreciate the depth of raga structures and the innovative way in which Sri Swamiji wove spiritual intention into each phrase. The concerts were not just an auditory experience but a spiritual darshan, as listeners experienced inner stillness and deep meditative states through the music. The Mumbai concerts reinforced the fact that Sri Swamiji is not merely a composer or performer but a divine channel through whom the ancient wisdom of Nāda Brahman is expressed.

Equally memorable was the healing music event in 2004 (and again in 2008) at Sirifort Auditorium in New Delhi, where Sri Swamiji addressed an audience comprising not only devotees and spiritual seekers but also dignitaries, scientists,

---

38. Carnatic and Hindustani music are the two major traditions of Indian classical music, each with distinct styles, histories, and aesthetics:

Carnatic Music

Origin: Southern India

Structure: Highly structured and composition-based

Key Elements: Kriti, Varnam, devotional themes

Improvisation: Within strict frameworks

Composers: Tyagaraja, Muthuswami Dikshitar, Shyama Shastri

Instruments: Veena, Mridangam, Violin, Flute

Hindustani Music

Origin: Northern India

Structure: Emphasizes improvisation and exploration of raga

Key Elements: Alap, Bandish, Taan

Influences: Persian and Islamic musical traditions

Gharanas (schools): Multiple stylistic lineages

Instruments: Sitar, Tabla, Sarod, Harmonium

In essence, Carnatic is more composition-driven and devotional, while Hindustani is more improvisational and expansive. Both aim for spiritual elevation through sound.

and scholars. This concert was particularly important because it coincided with efforts to bridge spiritual science with modern health paradigms. The music served as a living demonstration of the concepts of naḍī shuddhi (cleansing of energy channels), chakra or cakra balancing, and emotional recalibration through sound. It was a spiritually charged event that showcased how sacred music can be a tool for both individual and collective healing.

Perhaps one of the most unusual and symbolically profound events was the Pelham Caverns concert, which was not held in formal concert halls but in the natural echo chambers of caves in and around Tennessee, USA. Here, the healing music took on an elemental quality, blending with the subterranean silence to create a soundscape that was at once primeval and transcendent. The caves served as natural amplifiers of nāda, and Sri Swamiji's music, performed in such settings, evoked deep meditative stillness. These concerts were not widely publicized, and yet those who attended considered them among the most powerful of Sri Swamiji's healing sessions. They offered a return to the womb of nature, where the human soul could resonate with the Earth's deep silence and the cosmic sound of Sri Swamiji's voice and instruments.

On August 3, 2024, the subterranean expanse of The Caverns in Pelham, Tennessee, became the setting for a profound musical event: 'Guru Guha Raga Sagara,' led by His Holiness Sri Swamiji. This concert was part of Sri Swamiji's renowned Music for Meditation and Healing series, marking the first time such an event was held within a massive cave system. The natural acoustics and serene ambiance of The Caverns provided an unparalleled environment for this spiritual gathering. The term 'Guru Guha' holds deep significance. In Sanskrit, 'Guha' translates to 'cave,' symbolizing the heart or the innermost self. 'Guru Guha' is also a revered name for Lord Subrahmanya, representing the divine teacher residing within. By choosing this title, Sri Swamiji emphasized the journey inward, guiding attendees toward self-realization and inner peace through the medium of sacred music. The concert attracted a diverse audience of 1,300 individuals over two days, all seeking solace and healing through the transformative power of sound. Sri Swamiji's compositions, rooted in ancient ragas, were meticulously selected to resonate with the subtle energies of the human system, facilitating meditation and promoting holistic well-being.

The Caverns, renowned for hosting unique musical events, offered an environment where the boundaries between performer and audience dissolved, allowing the music to permeate deeply into the consciousness of all present. Attendees reported profound experiences, noting heightened states of meditation, emotional release, and a deep sense of tranquility. Sri Swamiji's pioneering integration of ancient musical traditions within such a distinctive natural setting underscored the timeless relevance of sound as a medium for healing and spiritual growth. The Guru Guha Raga Sagara concert not only honored the rich heritage of Indian devotional music but also demonstrated its universal appeal and capacity to unite individuals across cultures in the shared pursuit of inner harmony.

Across all these events, what remains consistent is the spiritual intentionality that underpins every concert. Each composition is chosen not merely for musical effect but for its vibrational signature. Sri Swamiji uses the keyboard, synthesizers, and supporting traditional instruments not to modernize Indian music but to create layers of sound that reach multiple strata of consciousness simultaneously. The presence of devotees during the concerts further amplifies the effect, as collective bhakti creates a field of heightened receptivity. These concerts are not passive entertainments—they are meditative immersions, healing journeys, and spiritual transmissions.

The global Music for Meditation and Healing events by Sri Ganapathy Sachchidananda Swamiji are thus unique in their integration of sacred intention, musical brilliance, therapeutic purpose, and universal accessibility. Whether it is the hallowed halls of Royal Albert or the natural acoustics of a cave, Sri Swamiji transforms each space into a sanctum of inner silence, proving time and again that sound—when consecrated by a realized being—can truly heal, awaken, and transform.

Let me now briefly mention a 'Night of Healing at Carnegie Hall' in New York when Sri Swamiji gifted a delectable musical treat for the soul to the select audience. On December 2, 2023, the world-famous Carnegie Hall in New York City witnessed something truly extraordinary—a concert not just of music but of healing and peace. Sri Swamiji performed His signature 'Atma Shanti[39] Raga Sagara,' a powerful concert of healing ragas dedicated to the victims and families affected by 9/11. The atmosphere was electric yet deeply meditative. Devotees and music lovers had flown in from across the world to experience this one-of-a-kind musical offering. As Sri Swamiji played soothing, healing ragas on his synthesizer, the audience sat in silent awe—some meditating, some with tears, and some even drifting into peaceful sleep, just as Sri Swamiji had lovingly instructed.

Joining Him on stage was violin maestro Dr L. Subramaniam, along with a stellar ensemble of artists—Jaitra Varanasi, Shankar Ramesh, Tanmoy Bose, Mani Narasimham, and Chandan Kumar. Together, they created a soundscape that was less performance and more a spiritual journey. The concert featured rare and specially curated ragas like Pranavaswarupam-Rushyaketupriya, Maayaroopa-Kaashyapi, Ishapateesha-Mohana, and Shambho Saamba-Hemavathi, each aimed at specific ailments—from

39. Atma Shanti: Peace of the soul.

cervical spondylosis and thyroid issues to insomnia, anxiety, and blood pressure problems. It wasn't just music—it was Nāda Chikitsa, or sound healing, in its purest form.

Representatives from the Indian Consulate and leaders from key charities like Wounded Warriors, Friends of Firefighters, EMS-FDNY Help Fund, and the NYC Veterans Administration attended and received donation cheques from the proceeds of the concert. These heartfelt moments, filled with gratitude, brought tears and smiles across the room.

Organized by Yoga Sangeeta, the nonprofit organization started by a group of devotees to do the music related works of Sri Swamiji in 2009 to promote healing music, the concert was also supported by Datta Yoga Center USA. Elmhurst Hospital's CEO Helen Arteaga added her presence, honoring Sri Swamiji's contribution to global well-being. In the end, it was not just a concert. It was a divine transmission of peace, a celebration of unity, and a profound reminder that music—when offered with pure intent—can truly heal the world.

The therapeutic potential of music, thus, has been recognized across cultures and epochs, serving as a testament to its profound impact on human health and well-being. Contemporary research and international experiences have further elucidated the multifaceted ways in which music facilitates healing, encompassing physical, emotional, and cognitive domains. In the realm of mental health, music has emerged as a potent adjunct to traditional therapeutic modalities. Classical pianist James Rhodes[40] advocates for the integration of music into

40. Classical pianist James Rhodes has been a vocal advocate for integrating music into mental health care, drawing from his personal experiences with trauma and recovery. In his 2015 memoir, *Instrumental: A Memoir of Madness, Medication, and Music*, Rhodes details the severe sexual abuse he endured during childhood and how classical music played a pivotal role in his healing process. He describes music as a 'pure good' that provided solace during his darkest times. Rhodes has

mental health care, suggesting that it can serve as an alternative or complement to medication in managing conditions such as depression and anxiety. Rhodes emphasizes that music possesses therapeutic power, potentially rivaling conventional treatments for certain individuals. His personal experiences underscore music's capacity to alleviate symptoms of anxiety and insomnia, offering solace and emotional release.

Neurological studies have demonstrated that music can significantly enhance cognitive functions, particularly in individuals with neurodegenerative disorders. For example, a study conducted by Yale University explored the effects of Latin dance music on seniors, aiming to assess its potential in delaying or preventing the onset of dementia. Participants

---

also explored the therapeutic potential of music in various media projects. In the 2013 Channel 4 series *Notes from the Inside*, he performed classical pieces for patients in psychiatric hospitals, aiming to offer comfort and connection through music. Reflecting on this experience, he noted that playing music in such settings could 'tunnel in through those meds,' suggesting a unique ability of music to reach individuals beyond pharmaceutical interventions.

THE INDEPENDENT

In a 2015 article for The Guardian, Rhodes challenges the stereotype of the 'mad composer' and emphasizes the beneficial link between music and mental well-being. He argues that while composers may have faced personal struggles, their creativity was not necessarily a product of mental illness and that music itself can be a therapeutic outlet for many.

THE GUARDIAN

Additionally, Rhodes's 2025 album, *Manía,* is conceived as a musical prescription for mental health, featuring works selected for their therapeutic properties. He believes that music can serve as an effective complement or alternative to medication in managing mental health conditions.

FINANCIAL TIMES

Through his writings, performances, and recordings, James Rhodes continues to advocate for the integration of music into mental health care, highlighting its profound capacity to heal and connect.

exhibited improvements in balance, attention, cognitive flexibility, and processing speed, highlighting music's role in bolstering both physical and mental faculties.

Music therapy has also shown promise in pain management. Research from McGill University indicates that personalized music, particularly tunes that align with an individual's natural tempo, can significantly reduce pain perception. This personalized approach underscores the importance of tailoring musical interventions to individual preferences and physiological responses, thereby enhancing the efficacy of music as a therapeutic tool.

Furthermore, music's capacity to evoke autobiographical memories has been harnessed in therapeutic settings, particularly for individuals with Alzheimer's disease. Music-evoked autobiographical memories (MEAMs) have been shown to improve mood, enhance memory retrieval, and foster social interactions among patients, thereby improving their overall quality of life. The integration of music into postoperative care has yielded notable benefits. A study presented at the American College of Surgeons revealed that patients who listened to music after surgery required significantly less morphine, experienced lower pain scores, reduced anxiety, and had decreased heart rates, all of which contributed to improved recovery outcomes.

The global recognition of music's therapeutic potential has led to its incorporation into mainstream healthcare practices. Music therapy is now utilized to address a variety of ailments, including chronic pain, depression, anxiety, Parkinson's, and Alzheimer's diseases. This integration signifies a paradigm shift towards more holistic approaches in medicine, acknowledging the profound connection between art and healing.

In conclusion, international experiences and scientific research collectively affirm that music possesses intrinsic healing properties. Its application across diverse therapeutic contexts underscores its versatility and efficacy as a non-pharmacological intervention, enriching the tapestry of global healthcare practices.

Healing Through Humility: Miracles and Music in the Lives of followers of Sri Ganapathy Sachchidananda Swamiji

I shall now try to explore the remarkable phenomena of healing, transformation, and life upliftment experienced by devotees of Sri Swamiji through His music, prayers, and divine grace. With characteristic humility, Sri Swamiji insists that all healing power belongs to Bhagawan Dattatreya, stating that He is only an instrument. His global initiative, Music for Meditation and Healing, blends ancient Nāda Chikitsa (sound healing) with classical ragas and modern synthesizer music to create vibrations that positively influence the human energy system. Testimonials abound of miraculous recoveries from illness, emotional relief, and reversal of professional and personal misfortunes—all attributed to Sri Swamiji's blessings. Rather than claim sole credit, Sri Swamiji encourages devotees to see His music as a supplement to, not a substitute for, conventional medical care. This section examines His musical methodology, global impact, and the philosophical underpinnings that guide His interventions, as well as narrating personal accounts from some devotees that exemplify how divine grace manifests through a living master's presence.

Sri Ganapathy Sachchidananda Swamiji's gentle smile radiates the humility at the heart of His healing philosophy. Ask Sri Swamiji about the extraordinary healings attributed to Him, and He will be the first to deflect credit. In satsangs and interviews, He often repeats that it is Bhagawan Dattatreya who heals—he is but an instrument. He has 'no separate will' of His own; instead, 'possessed by the Universal Divine current, He becomes an instrument of the Divine,' allowing a higher power to work through Him. This is not false modesty, but a lived creed—Sri Swamiji insists that any relief or miracle is the will of the Divine flowing through Him. He even observes that without divine sanction, He cannot intervene: sometimes He must simply watch a sufferer's pain 'because He has no orders from Datta…Mother Goddess does not permit' and if a person's karma demands they face hardship. In every healing prayer or musical offering, Sri Swamiji bows inwardly to that supreme source. For Him, God is the healer and He the channel, a stance that keeps Him ever humble even as devotees revere Him for life-changing cures.

This deep humility is matched by practical wisdom. Sri Swamiji never claims His music or blessings should replace medical care—in fact, He actively instructs devotees to continue their treatment. 'Music is not a substitute for medicines—it only potentiates them,' He states plainly. In His view, spiritual healing and modern medicine work in tandem, not in competition. Sri Swamiji sees His role as enhancing and accelerating healing, not solely delivering it. 'I only effect a rapport between man and God, the Supreme Reality, with help coming from man himself in good measure. I attune man to God through belief and music,' He says, describing how His interventions aim to spark a patient's own inner healing capacity alongside medical remedies. He often urges devotees to take their prescriptions and see their doctors but also listen with their hearts to the curative vibrations of divine music. In the gentle ambience of His ashram's prayer halls—incense lingering in the air, devotees seated in meditation—Sri Swamiji's bhajans and ragas become a sacred therapy to complement the pills and procedures. He has even established hospitals and medical camps as part of His mission, underscoring that caring for the body is as vital as caring for the soul. This blend of reverence and realism defines Sri Swamiji's approach: God's grace may heal, but one should never abandon the worldly means that God also provides.

If Sri Swamiji is the instrument, then music is the medium through which divine healing flows. His globally acclaimed initiative, Music for Meditation and Healing, narrated above, rests on the ancient idea of Nāda Chikitsa—healing through sound. In yoga traditions, the human body is more than flesh and bone; it is a vibration, an energy field threaded with nadis (subtle nerves) and anchored by spinning chakras (energy centers). Each nadi and chakra vibrate to certain frequencies. Sri Swamiji teaches that the right musical notes can retune these vibrations, like a musician tuning the strings of a veena. 'Music soothes the nadis and helps them vibrate at the proper rate,' He explains, and a balanced vibration, in turn, brings peace to body and mind. Fast or erratic vibrations (as in stress or illness) can be calmed by the 'unspoiled sounds of eternal nature' that ragas represent. In other words, sound is harnessed as medicine.

To deliver this sonic therapy, Sri Swamiji became a one-of-a-kind maestro. He has mastered dozens of classical Indian ragas—melodic scales, each imbued with a distinct mood and effect—and discovered through deep experimentation which raga can help which ailment. 'A great master understands the varying vibrational qualities of different ragas and knows which raga can help cure a particular disease,' Sri Swamiji's followers explain. For example, He might choose a serene raga in the early morning to ease anxiety or an upbeat raga at twilight to uplift someone from depression. Timing matters, too, as certain ragas are most potent at specific hours of the day. In concerts (more than 350 and counting) , He often announces the name and purpose of each raga—whether it is meant to strengthen one's heart or soothe the nerves or awaken spiritual energy. Decades ago, Sri Swamiji re-invented the term 'Raga Ragini Vidya' for this mystical science of ragas and their curative powers. Through long research, He even mapped ragas to elements of nature: planetary positions, colors, crystals, and herbs, finding an intricate interconnectedness between musical tones and the cosmos. The core idea is simple yet profound: 'Each note corresponds to one nerve,' so the melody that can touch that nerve can influence the organ or emotion linked to it. When the right notes resound, they stimulate dormant nerve centers and align the body's energy flow—much like acupuncture with sound instead of needles.

Sri Swamiji's concerts are, therefore, more than entertainment; they are healing sessions, often called 'Raga Sagara' (Ocean of Ragas) gatherings. Seated on stage in His flowing red robe, Sri Swamiji conjures a sonic ocean using a decidedly modern instrument—the electronic synthesizer. Traditionalists might expect a harmonium or sitar, but Sri Swamiji pioneered the use of the synthesizer for its remarkable range. This single instrument can mimic the tones of '1,008 different instruments,' He notes, giving Him an entire orchestra at his fingertips. 'I use devotional music as a means of spiritual energy transmission,' Sri Swamiji says, and the synthesizer (which He affectionately calls His 'modern veena') lets Him weave together layers of sound tailored to each audience. A deep bass drone might underpin a delicate flute-like melody; a rush of string sounds might imitate a thunderstorm one moment and birdsong the next. The result is a lush soundscape that envelops listeners. By reducing the need for many accompanists, the synthesizer also ensures that the healing vibrations remain focused and precise—an extension of Sri Swamiji's own sankalpa (spiritual intent) as He plays. Still, Sri Swamiji often shares the stage with renowned classical artists (violinists, tabla players, etc.), blending their live performances with His synthesized tones. The fusion of ancient ragas and modern technology in these concerts has captivated audiences from India to Europe and America.

Indeed, over the past four decades, Sri Swamiji has carried His Music for Meditation and Healing around the world. What began as a local experiment has grown into a globe-trotting mission. Since the 1980s, he has performed healing concerts in more than 30 countries, totalling over 350 performances. He has filled grand venues (mentioned earlier)—the Lincoln Center in New York, Royal Albert Hall in London, the Esplanade in Singapore, and even the storied Carnegie Hall—with seekers eager to experience His unique music. His initiative is now internationally recognized and even record-breaking. In 2015, Guinness World Records acknowledged Sri Swamiji for leading the largest music therapy lesson at the Sydney Opera House, where thousands gathered to learn and be healed by sound. During that event, Sri Swamiji explained the 'synergistic role of music in improving the outcome of the cure for chronic ailments, when complemented with medical treatment,' drawing connections between musical vibrations and the human nervous system. Medical professionals in the audience were struck by how elegantly He bridged science and spirituality. He described in detail the 'intricate relationship between nerves, sound vibrations, human organs' and how specific tones can impact particular nerve centers in the body. Such explanations have lent credibility to His music therapy work, even inspiring research: hospitals have begun playing His recordings in intensive care units, and studies have been initiated to examine the effects of His ragas on stress and the immune system. By marrying ancient Nāda Yoga concepts with modern therapeutic practice, Sri Swamiji has carved out a unique place as a healer-musician. As one Consul General who attended a concert observed, Sri Swamiji's approach 'has the potential to work wonders by harnessing profound healing capabilities' in a way that complements contemporary medicine. From intimate ashram gatherings to massive open-air 'Raga Sagara' concerts, the message is the same: music is a divine language of healing, and when one listens with total concentration ('with your heart and not with your intellect' as Sri Swamiji urges), the results can be transformative.

Harmonies of Healing: Stories of Transformation

The true measure of Sri Swamiji's music is in the testimonies of devotees whose lives have been touched by it. And these stories abound—circulating in ashram halls, printed in devotee memoirs, even noted by skeptical observers. One of the earliest and most famous accounts dates back about forty years and is often recounted as the origin story of Sri Swamiji's healing music. In the mid-1970s, a German devotee suffering from terminal cancer came to Sri Swamiji. Doctors had given up hope, and as a last resort, this man sought solace in His music. Sri Swamiji seated him nearby and began to play—different ragas in different tempos, carefully directed at the root cause of the illness. In the ensuing days, against all medical expectations, the man's condition improved, and ultimately, his cancer was declared in remission. Sri Swamiji's followers regard this as divine grace in action, triggered through the power of sound. He himself took it as a sign: if the correct musical vibrations are applied with sincere concentration, even 'incurable' maladies can potentially be healed by God's mercy. The German devotee's cure became a watershed moment. 'Equipped with this knowledge,' Sri Swamiji embarked on His worldwide healing concerts thereafter, confident that the ragas could carry Bhagawan Dattatreya's healing energy to countless others. Over the years, devotees and even curious newcomers have reported relief from a spectrum of ailments simply by attending these concerts or listening to His recordings. High blood pressure stabilizing, chronic back and joint pains easing, migraines and insomnia disappearing, memory loss in elders slowing, even children on the autism spectrum becoming calm and communicative—such testimonials pour in from all corners of the world. While each individual's experience is unique, the common refrain is that Sri Swamiji's music rekindled their vitality when nothing else did.

Not all of the healings are physical, and not all occur in the concert hall. Many occur in the quiet of Sri Swamiji's temple or even from afar through prayer and blessing. Mental and emotional suffering has been soothed in His presence like a fever broken by a cool breeze. Devotees speak of intense anxieties lifted after Sri Swamiji simply glanced at them or touched their foreheads with vibhuti (sacred ash). 'In the company of Sri Swamiji, what would heal the disturbed mind is not a verbal lecture or counseling...but the untainted, undiluted, spontaneous flow of His divine energy penetrating all those who come within His orbit,' one publication notes. To sit near Him in meditation is to feel a wave of peace silence the mind's turmoil. Even deep grief and depression have been alleviated. For instance, following a devastating personal loss, a devotee attended one of Sri Swamiji's meditation sessions; she later described that as Sri Swamiji chanted softly, she felt a heavy weight lifting from her chest for the first time since her tragedy. Such experiences are hard to quantify, but they are lifesaving to those who undergo them—a distressed mind 'healed by silence' or by a gentle bhajan where therapy and prayer become one.

Some devotee stories border on the miraculous. A middle-aged man from South India, for example, suffered persistent and mysterious stomach problems for years. Doctors and medicines had failed to cure his debilitating pain and digestive distress. Skeptical by nature, he was not one to seek out gurus. But as his condition worsened, desperation drove him to visit Sri Swamiji's ashram in Myṣuru. There, during a darshan, Sri Swamiji approached him with a knowing smile and spoke directly of the man's illness—startling him since he had told no one. 'Don't worry about your stomach problems,' Sri Swamiji said kindly. 'With the help of doctors and medicines, you could not cure your ailment, but then you wondered if Sri Swamiji could help. That very thought brought you here. Diseases and suffering are not meaningless; they have a great purpose. They are God-sent agents to cure man's real sickness, which is his lack of faith. So have faith…have faith.' These words penetrated the man's heart. In that moment, as he later recounted, a lifelong cynicism melted away, and he felt an overwhelming trust in God—a spiritual rebirth. He returned home with renewed hope. In the days and weeks that followed, this devotee found that his chronic symptoms gradually subsided until, to his astonishment, he was essentially cured. More astonishing to him was the inner change: 'I got tremendous relief for my long-standing stomach issues, and I realized that Sri Swamiji's unseen hands were behind all these changes in my life.' Not only was his body healing, but his whole lifestyle shifted—he lost interest in trivial pastimes and turned to bhajans and the *Bhagavad Gita* as if the illness had been a catalyst for both physical and spiritual transformation. It was as though Sri Swamiji had healed his soul first; the body simply followed. Stories like this have made the rounds among devotees, each told with tears of gratitude and a sense of awe. Skeptics may question coincidences or placebo effects, but to the devotees, the way everything unfolded—the 'accidental' visit to the ashram, Sri Swamiji addressing the very ailment unprompted, the steady recovery—feels like anything but coincidence. They see it as divine intervention through the Guru's grace.

'Invisible Hands': Grace in Worldly Affairs

The impact of Sri Swamiji's blessings is not confined to illness or mental anguish. Devotees also attribute to Him the removal of countless personal and professional obstacles that had hindered their progress in life. In hushed, reverent tones, they share testimonies of how Sri Swamiji's invisible hand seemed to guide them through crises of career and family, opening doors that had long been shut. A young engineer, for instance, might recall how, after receiving Sri Swamiji's teertham (holy water) and a single encouraging phrase from him, she suddenly landed a promotion that had been elusive for years. A businessman struggling with a failing enterprise finds that after Sri Swamiji's brief visit to his office, new opportunities and clients mysteriously start pouring in, reviving his fortunes. These devotees firmly believe it is Sri Swamiji's grace that orchestrates the turnaround, not mere luck.

One striking account comes from a devotee in Louisiana, USA—an entrepreneur who openly credits Sri Swamiji for the dramatic growth of his small business. In the late 1980s, this man's company was on the brink of collapse: his warehouse was nearly empty, and finances were in the red. When Sri Swamiji visited his town, the devotee invited Sri Swamiji to bless his struggling workplace. Sri Swamiji walked through the sparse warehouse and then sat at the man's desk. In a playful yet symbolic gesture, Sri Swamiji asked for a few coins—receiving three quarters—and tossed them into an empty drawer. 'Where do you keep your money for the business?' He had casually inquired; the embarrassed devotee admitted he had none. 'If you ever get money, where would you put it?' Sri Swamiji teased, then declared with a smile, 'Watch how these will grow.' He shut the drawer with the three coins inside as the devotee chuckled nervously at the idea. But indeed, what followed borders on the incredible. In the ensuing months, the man's fledgling business began to flourish. Contracts that had been stalled came through. Income increased exponentially. Within a short time, the empty warehouse was filled with activity and inventory. 'That money blessing really helped. My business grew tremendously, and I benefited a lot from His blessings,' the devotee attests even years later. He never forgot the image of those three coins in the drawer—a physical metaphor for the wealth and success that manifested seemingly out of nowhere. In his gratitude, this devotee built a small temple in his city on Sri Swamiji's instructions, feeling that his prosperity was by Sri Swamiji's design, not his own savvy. 'I figured that this was His money, and I was just the medium…I was awake to do whatsoever was His will,' he explains, describing himself as an instrument for Sri Swamiji just as Sri Swamiji is an instrument for the Divine. This humble attitude—that he was merely a caretaker of blessings—only seemed to invite more abundance, both material and spiritual. By Sri Swamiji's grace, he says, 'Two things happened to me: financially, I was better, and spiritually, I became better.'

Such stories illustrate what devotees view as Sri Swamiji's invisible guidance in their worldly lives. Whether it's finding a good job, resolving a family dispute, or succeeding in an academic endeavor, devotees often spy on the subtle fingerprints of His grace. Sometimes, Sri Swamiji gives direct advice or a cryptic instruction that later proves prescient. Other times, the devotee simply prays to His photo, and unexpectedly, 'coincidental' help arrives. To the outside eye, it may look like coincidence or the psychological boost of faith, but devotees experience it as something more—a kind of divine synchronicity engineered by their Sadguru.

Significantly, Sri Swamiji himself discourages any superstition or over-reliance on miracle-mongering. He reminds followers that life will still demand their effort and that His blessings are not magic wands. In fact, He often tests devotees' patience and commitment as if to ensure they do not become passive. For example, when the Louisiana devotee eagerly offered all his savings at Sri Swamiji's feet in thanks, Sri Swamiji handed it back, saying, 'I just wanted to test your willingness to give. You keep it and use it wisely'—teaching that one shouldn't expect the guru to simply solve everything without one's own responsibility. Sri Swamiji's blessings, as devotees come to learn, usually work in tandem with the devotee's own faith and action. They describe it as a spark that ignites their clarity, confidence, and determination. Once that inner fire is lit, obstacles that once loomed large begin to melt away almost of their own accord—or rather, by the guru's hidden hand. In this way, what appears miraculous is also perfectly natural: God helps those who help themselves, and Sri Swamiji's grace inspires devotees to help themselves with a newfound conviction that the Divine is backing them.

At the same time, there is an undeniable element of serendipity that devotees cherish as proof of Sadguru's hand in destiny. A family searching for a house finds the perfect home after Sri Swamiji blesses a piece of fruit for them. A student fearful of failing an exam receives a mantra from Sri Swamiji and then passes with top marks, saying later that an unexplainable calm and focus came during the test. A couple longing for a child is blessed by Sri Swamiji—he gives a flower prasadam—and soon after, they joyously conceive despite years of infertility. Such accounts, shared in letters and at prayer meetings, reinforce among devotees the sense that no aspect of life is too small or too big for Sri Swamiji's grace. It is not about superstition or treating Sri Swamiji like a wish-fulfilling genie; in fact, He often warns devotees against approaching gurus with transactional mindsets.

Rather, devotees have learned that when they surrender an issue to Sri Swamiji—truly let go of their worry and trust His guidance—something shifts in the universe to bring about a resolution, often in the most unexpected way. They see this as the Divine acting with Sri Swamiji as the facilitator aligning the cosmic forces in their favor.

In all these narratives of healing and obstacle removal, a striking theme emerges: Sri Swamiji's blessings are a catalyst, not a crutch. He kindles hope where there is despair and faith where there is doubt. Those sparks then illuminate the path forward for the devotee, who suddenly finds the strength or the lucky break needed to overcome the challenge. Sri Swamiji frequently emphasizes that God's grace works in proportion to one's sincerity. Thus, He doesn't advertise miracles or guarantee outcomes—what He gives is an impetus, a sacred push. Many times, He has said that the real miracle is the transformation of the devotee's heart and mindset. Once that inner transformation occurs, outer results naturally flow. A cured illness, a promotion at work, a healed relationship—these are outward signs of an inward shift ignited by contact with the Sadguru.

And so, devotees revere Sri Ganapathy Sachchidananda Swamiji in a dual light: as a compassionate healer who can channel divine love to mend body and mind and as a benevolent guide who quietly clears the karmic obstacles from their life's journey. In their eyes, both forms of grace spring not from the man alone but from the Divinity He represents. Sri Swamiji Himself remains ever humble, reminding all that He is merely 'the flute, not the flute-player.' The music of healing that flows through Him, He insists, is the breath of Bhagawan Dattatreya. This beautiful humility only deepens devotees' faith. They see in Sri Swamiji a living bridge between the human and the Divine—a bridge over which compassion, healing, and miracles travel freely in one direction and prayers, love, and gratitude travel in the other. The narrative of His life's work is thus a racy yet reverent symphony: a Guru who plays cosmic melodies to alleviate suffering, a servant of God who attributes every success to that God, and a friend to thousands who kindles the light of hope in their darkest moments. Each time a life is transformed—be it a cancer remitted, a mind restored to peace, or a career uplifted—devotees celebrate it as Bhagawan Datta's healing touch made manifest through the gentle hands of their beloved Sri Swamiji. And as the chorus of 'Jaya Guru Datta' rises in the ashram, one senses that this interplay of divine grace and guru's love will continue to inspire and heal countless hearts for generations to come.

The life and work of Sri Ganapathy Sachchidananda Swamiji stand as a radiant testament to the power of humility, faith, and divine music. Through His repeated assertion—'It is Datta who heals, I am only an instrument'—Sri Swamiji not only redirects attention to the Supreme but models the sacred detachment of a true yogi and Avadhoota. His healing concerts and therapeutic music have touched thousands across the globe, blending the subtle science of ragas with the deep vibrations of compassion and Sankalpa[41] Shakti. Devotees across continents testify to recoveries from illness, success in personal and professional life, and above all, a profound inner peace born from contact with the Master. Yet, Sri Swamiji never promotes miracles or promises magical cures. Instead, He kindles within each seeker a trust in divine timing and personal transformation. His healing is not just of the body—it is of the soul, gently leading devotees from suffering toward surrender, from disquiet to devotion. In the harmonies of His music and the serenity of His smile, seekers find not just a guru

41. Sankalpa: a solemn vow, intention or resolve often used in yogic practices to set a heartfelt intention that aligns with one's highest truth.

but a bridge to the Divine. Thus, in the raga of life, Sri Swamiji plays the note that restores balance, awakens spirit, and invites all to experience the sublime presence of Datta through sound, grace, and surrender.

References

1. *Music as Medicine* by Daniel Levitin; www.ft.com; www.commonwealthclub.org;www.goodreads.com; wwwtheguardian.com
2. www.ctinsider.com
3. www.nypost.com
4. www.emtc-eu.com; European Music Therapy Confederation
5. www.musictherapysource.com: Music Therapy Schools International
6. www.sgsragasagara.com
7. www.esmuc.cat
8. www.dattapeetham.org
9. Mr Vishnudatta Jayaraman's post in www.dattapeetham.org and www.yogasangeeta.org
10. Sri Ganapathy Sachchidananda Swamiji discourses and official publications.
11. Avadhoota Datta Peetham archives on Music Therapy and healing miracles.
12. First-hand devotee experience narratives (SGS Puttugam series).
13. News reports on Swamiji's music therapy initiatives and global concerts.

CHAPTER 5

Sacred Resonance: The Transformative Power of Sri Ganapathy Sachchidananda Swamiji's Music

(Review of an Article by Bill Osmer[42] in December 2006 on www.dattapeetham.com)

Abstract

This chapter reviews the unique and profound significance of the music of Sri Ganapathy Sachchidananda Swamiji, as assessed by Bill Osmer

42. In December 2006, Bill Osmer authored a comprehensive paper titled 'Raga Chikitsa and Raga Ragini Vidya,' delving into the therapeutic applications of Indian classical music. In this work, Osmer explores how specific ragas can influence the body's energy centers (chakras), elements, and pathways (naḍīs), thereby promoting healing and well-being. He attributes the revival and development of these ancient musical healing techniques to his guru, Sri Ganapathy Sachchidananda Swamiji of the Avadhoota Datta Peetham in Mysuru, India. Osmer emphasizes that Sri Swamiji's method integrates various ancient sciences, including astrology, gemology, astronomy, herbology, mantra science, chromotherapy, crystal therapy, and Ayurveda, into the healing process. Through intuitive insights and extensive research, Sri Swamiji has correlated the 72 melakarta ragas with specific chakras, elements, naḍīs, planets, and astrological signs, providing profound implications for the therapeutic aspects of music from an Ayurvedic perspective.

in December 2006, through a spiritual, therapeutic, and philosophical lens. The music of Sri Swamiji is not merely an artistic or devotional expression but a living embodiment of Nāda Brahma—the Divine as sound. Drawing from ancient Indian traditions such as Nāda Chikitsa and Raga Ragini Vidya, Sri Swamiji's music functions as a potent force for healing, emotional transformation, and spiritual awakening. The chapter reflects on how Sri Swamiji's compositions transcend linguistic, cultural, and intellectual boundaries to reach the soul of the listener, offering a direct experience of inner peace and divine presence. The discussion is framed within the context of modern scientific inquiry into the effects of music on the human brain while affirming that Sri Swamiji's music arises from yogic realization rather than theoretical understanding. Ultimately, this sacred music is portrayed as a form of darshan—a means of receiving the guru's grace and entering the field of divine vibration.

Sri Ganapathy Sachchidananda Swamiji's music represents a profound confluence of ancient spiritual tradition and modern therapeutic understanding. This music is far more than devotional or aesthetic expression—it is a calibrated, conscious act of healing and spiritual elevation, born from the deep experiential wisdom of a realized master. The music of Sri Swamiji is understood not simply as a composition of melodic sounds but as a living, vibrating force—Nāda Brahma—the Divine in the form of sound.

In evaluating the significance of Swamiji's music, one would see that Sri Swamiji does not merely perform music; rather, He channels divine vibrations through His voice and instruments to transform the inner landscape of the listener. Rooted in the Vedic and Yogic traditions of Nāda Chikitsa (healing through sound), Sri Swamiji's music is infused with specific ragas—melodic frameworks known to correspond with particular emotional and physiological states. Osmer notes that Sri Swamiji's knowledge of Raga Ragini Vidya (the science of melodic healing) is not academic or learned in the conventional sense but arises spontaneously from His deep meditative state and yogic insight.

What sets this music apart, in Osmer's view, is its direct capacity to touch and rewire the inner consciousness of the listener. He reflects that Sri Swamiji's music has the power to calm a restless mind, lift the veil of sorrow, and dissolve psychological burdens without the need for spoken words. In this light, the music becomes an extension of His divine compassion—an audible expression of His will to heal, uplift, and guide humanity. It bypasses the intellect and penetrates the heart, altering emotional frequencies and enhancing one's receptivity to spiritual truths.

Moreover, Osmer places Sri Swamiji's musical work within the emerging dialogue between science and spirituality, particularly referencing neuroscientific studies and the work of researchers like Daniel Levitin. While modern science investigates the therapeutic impact of sound and rhythm on the brain and nervous system, Sri Swamiji has long demonstrated these truths experientially in His concerts and spiritual gatherings. One needs to note that such scientific validation is not the basis of Sri Swamiji's authority; rather, it is the contemporary world's late discovery of truths that Sri Swamiji has lived and transmitted for decades.

The concerts of Sri Swamiji—often performed to large audiences across the world as described in earlier chapters—are collective healing events. The music produced in these gatherings creates a vibrational field that affects not only individual listeners but also the collective emotional and spiritual atmosphere. People from diverse backgrounds, languages, and cultures report similar effects of peace, transformation, and inner clarity after attending these events, which speaks to the universal resonance of this divine sound.

Finally, the significance of Sri Swamiji's music cannot be confined to scholarly analysis or musical critique. It is a sacred offering, an act of divine play (lila), and a manifestation of Sri Swamiji's inner silence expressed through sound. The music is not merely for entertainment or even for meditation—it is itself a form of darshan, a way of receiving the Guru's presence and grace. To hear this music is to be drawn into a sacred current that uplifts, purifies, and heals—not just the body or mind but the very soul of the listener.

The music of Sri Ganapathy Sachchidananda Swamiji stands as a rare and sacred phenomenon in today's world—a divine intersection of sound, silence, and spiritual healing. Far beyond the realm of entertainment or performance, it is an audible transmission of higher consciousness intended to uplift and transform all who encounter it. Sri Swamiji's music is a continuation of His mission to bring solace, clarity, and inner awakening to humanity. It reflects the ancient wisdom of the sages while responding to the contemporary need for emotional healing and spiritual anchoring. Whether experienced in the intimacy of solitude or in the charged atmosphere of a large healing concert, this music touches the listener at the deepest level, bypassing intellectual constructs and calling the soul home. Through His music, Sri Swamiji offers not just melody but a mirror to the Self, a balm for suffering, and a bridge to the eternal.

References

1. Avadhoota Datta Peetham. (n.d.). *Healing Through Music: Nāda Chikitsa and Sri Swamiji's Global Musical Mission*. Mysuru, India: Avadhoota Datta Peetham Publications. Retrieved from https://www.dattapeetham.org/page/view/bhajans-and-healing-music

2. Avadhoota Datta Peetham. (n.d.). *Sri Ganapathy Sachchidananda Swamiji's Musical Events and Raga Sagara Concerts.* Retrieved from https://www.dattapeetham.org/page/view/raga-sagara

3. Osmer, B. (2006, December). *Sacred Resonance: A Review of Sri Ganapathy Sachchidananda Swamiji's Healing Music.* Retrieved from https://www.dattapeetham.org (Archived article section – December 2006).

4. Sri Ganapathy Sachchidananda Swamiji. (2005). *Nāda Chikitsa: Healing Through Divine Sound.* Mysuru, India: Datta Peetham Publications.

5. Sri Ganapathy Sachchidananda Swamiji. (n.d.). *Nāda Brahma: The Sacred Sound of the Divine.* Audio teachings. Available at SGS Ashrama Archives.

6. Levitin, D.J. (2006). *This Is Your Brain on Music: The Science of a Human Obsession.* New York: Dutton/Penguin Books.

7. Sundar, A. (2012). *Spiritual Music and Contemporary Healing: The Case of Avadhoota Datta Peetham.* In Contemporary Hindu Spirituality (pp. 165–172). Delhi: Bharatiya Vidya Bhavan.

8. Sri Swamiji Music Archives. (n.d.). *Raga Ragini Vidya: Ancient Science of Melodic Healing as Practiced by Sri Swamiji.* Mysuru: Datta Peetham Media.

CHAPTER 6

How I Came in Contact with Sri Ganapathy Sachchidananda Swamiji

(Continuing from Chapter 2)

Abstract

Sri Ganapathy Sachchidananda Swamiji, revered globally for His spiritual guidance and mystical abilities, has been the focal point of numerous miraculous accounts as reported by His devotees. These narratives encompass a wide spectrum of experiences, including the awe-inspiring Agni Puja during Maha Shivaratri, instances of devotees being rescued from near-death situations, healing of chronic illnesses through His therapeutic music, and the removal of obstacles leading to success in professional and personal endeavors. This chapter delves into these extraordinary occurrences, drawing upon documented testimonials and publications by devotees to explore the profound impact of Sri Swamiji's divine interventions. I add my own experiences to the narrative to bring out the outcomes of the powerful blessings of Sri Swamiji.

Let me now come back to continuing my journey and how my association with Sri Swamiji developed after 1994 (where I left off in Chapter 2) till the present day. It is a long story spreading across 30 years. I will restrict my narration only to the most essential, remarkable, and memorable ones so that the chapter does not become a dreary read.

What are miracles? Did I or my family experience any miraculous events or incidents in our association with Sri Swamiji? But, before that, let me recount the gist of the experiences of thousands of devotees, which have been documented.

Divine Interventions: Miracles Attributed to Sri Ganapathy Sachchidananda Swamiji

Sri Ganapathy Sachchidananda Swamiji is celebrated not only for His spiritual teachings but also for the miraculous experiences attributed to His presence and practices. Devotees worldwide have shared numerous accounts of divine interventions, ranging from spectacular ritualistic events to personal transformations and healings. These narratives, documented in various publications, offer a glimpse into the profound influence Sri Swamiji has had on the lives of his followers. I have personally witnessed miraculous healing and recovery from sudden and serious ailments from scores of my friends and fellow devotees. Each of the persons and their families attribute the miraculous recovery to the grace and blessings of Sri Swamiji. Ailments that they recovered from ranged from lung cancer, severe lung infection and pneumonia, brain-related illnesses, and major life-threatening complications. Let me now come to very special instances where Sri Swamiji's miraculous powers have manifested themselves regularly in the form of Agni Puja during Maha Shivaratri[43] and the Nāda Chikitsa sessions.

---

43. Maha Shivaratri is a major Hindu festival dedicated to Lord Shiva, observed

The Agni Puja during Maha Shivaratri

One of the most renowned events associated with Sri Swamiji is the Agni Puja (fire worship) performed during Maha Shivaratri. This sacred fire ritual, conducted in the presence of thousands of devotees, is believed to invoke divine energies and blessings. Witnesses have reported experiencing an overwhelming sense of spiritual elevation and purification during the ceremony. The intense heat of the fire, coupled with Sri Swamiji's serene composure, has been described as a testament to His mastery over the elements and His deep connection with the Divine. These experiences have been chronicled in various devotee publications, highlighting the transformative power of the Agni Puja. The Pratyaksha Agni Puja, a sacred fire worship conducted on the auspicious occasion of Maha Shivaratri, involves intricate Vedic ceremonies centered around the consecrated fire, symbolizing the divine presence of Lord Shiva. During the puja, Sri Swamiji would offer oblations into the fire while chanting powerful mantras, creating a spiritually charged atmosphere that deeply resonated with devotees. The puja was not merely a ritualistic practice but a profound spiritual experience, emphasizing purity of purpose, unwavering devotion, and noble conduct. Sri Swamiji emphasized that such worship should be performed with total purity of purpose, single-minded devotion, and sterling nobility in thought, word, and deed. This approach enabled Him to engage in the Agni Puja, offering worship and, most miraculously, emerging unscathed. This has since been discontinued for the last decade or so on the repeated imploring by 'concerned' devotees.

---

annually with night-long vigils, fasting, chanting of mantras, and offerings to the Shiva Linga. It symbolizes the overcoming of darkness and ignorance, and is believed to be the night when Shiva performed the cosmic dance of creation, preservation, and destruction.

Rescue from Near-Death Experiences

Numerous devotees have recounted (and continue to recount) instances where they believe Sri Swamiji's intervention saved them from life-threatening situations. For example, there are stories of individuals involved in severe accidents who, despite the odds, emerged unscathed after invoking Sri Swamiji's name or recalling His teachings. These accounts often emphasize a sudden, inexplicable turn of events that led to their survival, which they attribute to Sri Swamiji's protective grace. Such testimonials are prevalent in devotee literature, underscoring the profound faith followers place in His divine guardianship. We have felt this when our son Datta miraculously survived two near-fatal car accidents almost in the same vicinity of Lodi Road in South Delhi—which we attribute solely to the kindness and protection of Sri Swamiji.

Healing Through Music

Sri Swamiji's unique approach to healing through music, known as 'Music for Meditation and Healing,' has garnered significant attention (discussed in chapters 3 to 5 earlier). Devotees have reported experiencing relief from chronic ailments and psychological distress after attending His music sessions or listening to His compositions. The therapeutic effects of His music are believed to stem from the specific ragas and rhythms employed, which resonate with the body's energy centers to promote healing. Publications by devotees often include testimonials of miraculous recoveries and improved well-being attributed to Sri Swamiji's musical interventions. The latest experience was from first-time listeners of His 'Sasya Raksha Raga Sagara' Music for Meditation and Healing on March 22, 2025, in the South Asian Bonsai Federation in their Bliss 2025 event in the Convention Hall of Radisson Hotel, Karjat, Maharashtra, where Sri Swamiji was also the chief guest for the inauguration of the Conference. Scores of audience members, most of them foreigners (from USA, Singapore, Philippines, Japan, and South Korea), profusely thanked Sri Swamiji and narrated with goosebumps their experiences of ecstasy, peaceful mind, and deep relaxation they had in those 60 minutes of the session.

Removal of Obstacles and Success in Life

Many followers credit Sri Swamiji for removing personal and professional obstacles, leading to significant gains in their careers, businesses, wealth, and health. Devotees have shared stories of unexpected promotions, business turnarounds, and resolutions to long-standing personal issues following their association with Sri Swamiji. These experiences are often characterized by a series of serendipitous events or newfound clarity and confidence, which devotees believe are the result of Sri Swamiji's blessings and guidance.

My own numerous experiences in my career from 1991 till 2015 and, more so, thereafter till date are nothing short of miraculous. In my view, miracles do not mean the materialization of rings, pendants, chains, or similar other things. Where do I start?

After my London tenure of 1991–94, I was posted to another difficult place, Srinagar in Jammu & Kashmir (J&K), a second 'tough' posting (Kohima-London-Srinagar) in a career which is rather rare. J&K was going through a serious crisis of terrorism-linked violence at the time. We were to travel in a bulletproof car and with armed escort. I could come out of the posting in less than seven months because of the grace of Sri Swamiji, which is again a rarity, as at least one or two years would be the norm for such tenures. The next stint in Mumbai enabled me to organize, with Sri Swamiji's blessings, a Music for Meditation and Healing concert in Anushaktinagar, Bhabha Atomic Research Centre (BARC) Complex, on November 3, 1996, for which the chief guest was the Late Dr R. Chidambaram, then Chairman of Atomic Energy Commission and later Principal Scientific Adviser to the Government. Famous violinist Dr L. Subramanian, Dr Thiruvaroor Bhaktavatsalam (Mridangam), and Dr N. Ramani (Flute) accompanied Sri Swamiji. More than 5,000 people, most of them senior scientists, engineers and doctors who were first-time participants, attended and enjoyed the gift of musical offering of Sri Swamiji. Could I alone have coordinated or helped organize this mammoth event? It was the miracle of the blessings of Sri Swamiji that enabled the event to be conducted. I learned a number of things. The leadership of and responsibility taken up by my good friend, Mr T.K. Sankaranarayanan, a senior scientific officer of BARC and an acclaimed Carnatic music critic and aficionado—besides being the honorary secretary of the famous Bhakta Rasika Ranjani Sabha of Anushaktinagar—was fantastic without which the event would not have been possible to organize for an outsider to BARC. In fact, it is the miracle of Sri Swamiji that a person like Mr Sankaranarayanan, who was not a devotee of Sri Swamiji, was motivated to lead the event. He has very recently attended a Music for Meditation event in November 2024 in Sahyadri Hanuman Datta Kshetra (SHDK) in Chinchwan and continues to hold Sri Swamiji in great regard. For His part, Sri Swamiji has a unique fondness for Mr Sankaranarayanan, too, whom He has exhorted to organize another event.

This was followed by three more events in 1998, 1999, and 2000 in Shanmukhananda Hall, Fine Arts Society in Chembur, Matunga Gymkhana grounds, where Sri Swamiji gave me the opportunity to organize Music for Meditation and Healing concerts besides satsang and bhajans by Sri Swamiji.

I gratefully acknowledge the support rendered by my good friend and devotee of Sri Swamiji, Sri Nikhil J. Merchant, and his family in Mumbai in organizing each of these events.

A few days before I was transferred to New Delhi in 2001, my mother-in-law was diagnosed with breast cancer in Hyderabad. It was clearly His blessings that despite my transfer, her surgery and post-surgery treatment proceeded well, so much so that even now, when she is 88 years old, she has not only recovered from the dreaded ailment but continues to be independent and healthy for her age.

Some of my friends confronted me with a question. Why is it that my father-in-law, who was diagnosed with brain cancer around 2010, did not survive his surgery despite Sri Swamiji's blessings? It is true that he did not survive the disease, but we all agree that it was Sri Swamiji who gave him, his wife, and his daughter the strength to meet the difficult situation and the latter two to overcome the tragic loss soon enough. Sri Swamiji did pray for the soul, and we are satisfied that he reached the lotus feet of Sri Swamiji in the other world.

Even as recently as 2018, Sri Swamiji blessed my granddaughter (named by Him as Yamini), who had a heart-related ailment, and she is now normal. Similarly, Sri Swamiji blessed my grandson (named by Him as Gakara Datta in January 2025) profusely as doctors here had instilled fear about his alleged ventricular condition while my daughter-in-law (Saloni) was pregnant with him. In fact, two reputed gynecologists had clearly said that my daughter-in-law may have difficulties in conceiving on an earlier consultation. But Gakara happened. These are nothing short of miracles for us.

Coming to Delhi, Sri Swamiji gave me the opportunity to serve the causes dear to Him by organizing Music for Meditation and Healing events in the FICCI Auditorium, Sirifort Auditorium (twice), and Dwaraka from 2003 to 2015. Sri Swamiji also gave me the opportunity to organize the Kumbhabhishekam of Dattatreya in the temple in Swaroopnagar, New Delhi, in 2004. This deserves a special mention.

Kumbhabhishekam is a significant Hindu temple consecration ceremony aimed at sanctifying and invigorating the temple and its deities. The term combines 'Kumbha,' meaning a water pot, and 'Abhishekam,' which refers to the ritualistic pouring or sprinkling of sacred water. This elaborate ritual is integral to both the initial consecration of a new temple and the periodic re-consecration of existing ones, typically performed every 12 years to rejuvenate the spiritual energy believed to reside within the temple structures and idols.

The ceremony spans several days and encompasses a series of intricate rituals prescribed by the Agama Shastras, ancient scriptures that provide guidelines for temple construction and worship. The process begins with preliminary rites such as honoring Lord Ganesha—the remover of obstacles—and performing Bhumi Puja, a prayer to Mother Earth seeking her blessings and support for the temple. Priests undertake purification rituals, including tying protective threads (Raksha Bandhanam) and planting grains to symbolize fertility and prosperity.

The Agama Shastras are a vast collection of scriptures that serve as foundational texts for various spiritual traditions within Hinduism, particularly in Shaivism,[44] Vaishnavism,[45]

---

44. Shaivism is one of the major traditions within Hinduism that reveres Lord Shiva as the Supreme Being, emphasizing asceticism, devotion, and the cyclical nature of creation and destruction. It encompasses a wide range of philosophies and practices, from devotional worship (bhakti) to metaphysical schools like Kashmir Shaivism and Shaiva Siddhanta.

45. Vaishnavism is a major tradition within Hinduism that worships Lord Vishnu—and his avatars like Rama and Krishna—as the Supreme God who sustains and protects the universe. It emphasizes devotion (bhakti),

and Shaktism.[46] The term 'Agama' translates to 'that which has come down,' signifying teachings that have been handed down through generations. These texts are revered for their detailed expositions on theology, philosophy, meditation practices, ethical conduct, and elaborate guidelines for rituals and temple construction.

Each Agama is traditionally divided into four sections: Jnana Pada (Knowledge Section) – This segment delves into the philosophical and spiritual underpinnings of the tradition, exploring concepts of reality, the nature of the Divine, and the path to liberation; Yoga Pada (Meditation Section) – Focusing on the discipline of yoga, this section outlines practices for mental and physical control, aiming to prepare practitioners for spiritual enlightenment; Kriya Pada (Ritual Section) – Here, meticulous instructions are provided for performing rituals, constructing temples, and crafting idols, encompassing the procedural aspects of worship and the symbolic significance of various ritualistic elements; and Charya Pada (Conduct Section) – This part prescribes the ethical and moral codes of conduct for devotees and ascetics, detailing daily observances, rites, and the celebration of festivals.

The influence of the Agama Shastras is profound in shaping the liturgical and architectural traditions of Hindu temples. They provide comprehensive guidelines on the design and construction of temples, ensuring that every aspect, from the sanctum to the subsidiary shrines, adheres to sacred principles. This ensures that

righteousness, and the path to liberation through grace, often expressed through temple rituals, scriptures like the Bhagavad Gita, and devotional songs.

46. Shaktism is a prominent tradition within Hinduism that worships the Divine Mother or Shakti—the feminine cosmic energy—as the supreme power underlying all creation, preservation, and destruction. Devotees revere goddesses such as Durga, Kali, Lakshmi, and Saraswati, and emphasize rituals, tantra, and inner awakening as paths to spiritual liberation.

the temple serves as a microcosm of the universe, facilitating a deeper connection between the devotee and the Divine. While the Agamas share the Vedic spirit, they do not derive their authority directly from the Vedas. Instead, they are considered complementary, offering practical approaches to spirituality that are accessible to a broader segment of society. This inclusivity has contributed to the widespread adoption and enduring relevance of the Agama traditions in Hindu religious practice. The Agama Shastras encapsulate a rich tapestry of spiritual knowledge and practical guidance, playing a pivotal role in the preservation and perpetuation of Hindu religious traditions.

Central to the Kumbhabhishekam is the sanctification of water contained in numerous Kumbhas (sacred pots). These pots are meticulously arranged around a Yagasala, a temporary structure housing brick fire altars where priests conduct homas (fire sacrifices). Through the chanting of Vedic mantras and the performance of fire rituals, the water in these pots is believed to be infused with divine energy. On the auspicious day and time determined for the consecration, this sanctified water is ceremoniously poured over the temple's main tower (Gopuram) and the deities within the sanctum sanctorum, symbolizing the infusion of spiritual energy and the deity's presence into the idols. An essential aspect of the Kumbhabhishekam is the Ashtabandhanam, a process involving the affixing of the deity's idol to its pedestal using a paste made from eight specific herbs mixed with materials like wood lac, limestone powder, resin, red ochre, beeswax, and butter. This paste ensures the stability of the idol and is believed to maintain its sanctity and spiritual potency for a period of 12 years.

The culmination of the Kumbhabhishekam is marked by the Purnahuti, the final offering into the sacred fire, signifying the completion of the rituals. Priests then carry the sanctified Kumbhas in a grand procession around the temple, ascending to the temple's towers to pour the holy water over the structures and the assembled devotees below, thereby consecrating the entire temple complex and its surroundings. This sacred ceremony serves not only to sanctify the temple but also to unite the community, as devotees actively participate in the rituals, offerings, and festivities, reinforcing their collective spiritual commitment and cultural heritage.

Pujya Sri Swamiji made me the executive trustee of Sri Dattatreya Gnana Bodha Satsang Sabha Charitable Trust (SDGBSSCT) in 2019, which continues to date.

Could I have earned this singular honor and many others to follow but for the blessings and kindness of Sri Swamiji? Impossible. If these are not miracles, what else or more could I cite in support of my unbelievable experiences?

In all these endeavors, it is my wife, Usha, who has been singularly responsible for the unflinching support, liberal criticism, suggestions, guidance, monitoring, coordinating, and innovative inputs that enabled me to navigate the paths. If there is one matter or subject that my wife and I agree upon, it is the devotion to Sri Swamiji—honestly, my wife has far greater devotion and yearning to serve Sri Swamiji than me. Usha thinks, breathes, and lives for the causes of Sri Swamiji, and there is a lot that I need to learn and imbibe from her in this regard. It would not be an exaggeration to state that it is Usha who has been diligently and scrupulously monitoring and following up on the activities and events literally every day in both Delhi (SDGBSSCT) and Mumbai (SHDK) units of Avadhoota Datta Pertham.

Sri Swamiji has continued His kindness to me by nominating me as a trustee in the Sri Ganapathy Sachchidananda Avadhoota Datta Peetha Trust, Mysuru, in 2020. Sri Swamiji also entrusted me, earlier in 2019, with the responsibilities of managing the activities and proposed construction of temples of Karyasiddhi

Panchmukha Hanuman and Bhagawan Dattatreya in SGS Sahyadri Hanuman Datta Kshetra (SHDK) in Chinchwan village in Panvel, Raigad district in Maharashtra. It is His miraculous blessings that enabled me to obtain clearances or 'No Objection Certificates' from more than 50 government and semi-government agencies for the plans and layout of the proposed temple complex from state government authorities, which were mandatory before we could commence construction. My civil service friends helped me with moral support. This was despite the disruption caused by lockdowns, etc., due to the onset of the Covid pandemic. With His blessings, we could spread the message and promote the activities in the villagers of the area and continue various programs, including mass feeding or Anandan and teaching compositions (bhajans) of Sri Swamiji to the children of the villages. The unit became self-sufficient in 2024 after struggling for around ten years—all because of the blessings of Sri Swamiji.

I had another miraculous experience of helping (in a small way) organize the Kumbhabhishekam and installation of the Panchamukha Anjaneya Temple in the BHEL colony in Hyderabad in 2021. The organizers were facing some operational legacy issues and hurdles from some of the officials of the local BHEL management, and there was a court matter. While the judicial decision came in favor of the local trust, operationally, there were a few issues that needed to be tackled. A former CMD of BHEL, Sri B. Prasada Rao, went out of his way to understand the issue and then prevailed upon the local BHEL management to cooperate with the events. The program was arranged successfully. This could not have been possible without the silent blessings of Sri Swamiji, both to me and, especially, Sri Prasada Rao.

Sri Swamiji's countless and continued blessings on my family are the sole reason that we could continue on the path of rendering little seva or service in the promotion of the noble causes espoused by Him.

The myriad miraculous experiences attributed to Sri Ganapathy Sachchidananda Swamiji, as documented by His other longstanding devotees, reflect the profound impact of His spiritual presence and practices. From the awe-inspiring Agni Puja during Maha Shivaratri to personal accounts of healing, protection, and success, these narratives underscore the deep faith and reverence that followers have for Sri Swamiji. While these experiences are deeply personal and can be considered subjective by some, they collectively contribute to the rich tapestry of devotion and belief surrounding Sri Swamiji's life and work.

I would now like to add an exclusive section to this chapter, further amplifying my very personal experiences over the years in my association with Sri Swamiji. I would like to call the section 'Beyond Coincidence: Miracles and Meaning in My Journey with Sri Ganapathy Sachchidananda Swamiji.'

In a world driven by metrics and milestones, the presence of a living master can appear enigmatic to the rational mind. This section reflects on a deeply personal journey spanning decades of association with Pujya Sri Swamiji, exploring not just what has happened but how it happened—and, more importantly, why. Is there a possible answer to the question 'Why?'

Was it grace? Was it fate? Was it a coincidence? Through unexplained recoveries, improbable career transformations, and impossible accomplishments in both personal and professional life, this narrative unfolds a deeper understanding of what constitutes a miracle. It is not merely the postponement of death or the avoidance of suffering but the orchestration of life events in a manner so profound, so synchronous, that one is compelled to surrender the illusion of control and accept the presence of the Divine hand. At the same time, it wrestles with an important dilemma—does spiritual anchoring imply emotional fragility? Or is it, perhaps, the secret source of inner strength? These questions, once hurled at me by fair-minded peers and skeptical friends, have only deepened my conviction: that Sri Swamiji is not a crutch for the weak but the fulcrum of a life lived meaningfully.

'What exactly have you gained from your association with Sri Ganapathy Sachchidananda Swamiji?'

That question, sometimes asked with hushed curiosity and at other times with the sharp edge of skepticism, has followed me through my career and beyond. Friends, colleagues, and even fellow civil servants—rational, well-meaning individuals—have often wondered aloud: is it merely emotional comfort? A psychological anchor in times of distress? Or is there something deeper, something that defies explanation?

And I understand why they ask. In the civil services, where objectivity and empirical proof are currency, talk of miracles and divine intervention can sound like indulgences for the emotionally frail. 'We are all born to die,' they say, 'so how does surviving an illness or escaping a mishap become a miracle?' 'If your health improves with treatment, isn't it just good medicine?' Or even more pointedly, 'Does belief in a guru not make you mentally dependent?'

For a long time, I didn't rush to answer. Because I myself wasn't rushing for answers—I was watching the patterns.

In 2018, I experienced a disturbing and unexplained drop in hemoglobin levels—from 10 to 8—in a short span, accompanied by persistent and severe gastritis. CT scans, endoscopies, pathological tests—all were inconclusive. A few months of iron supplements and dietary changes seemed to fix the problem. So, was it a miracle or just an effective treatment? I would say both. Yes, medicine played a role, but something more subtle had shifted. I didn't panic; I didn't spiral into fear. Instead, I was steady, even strangely confident. Why? Because in the background of the suffering, there was an unshakeable calm, a reassurance that I was being held. That calm wasn't of my making—it was His.

But if this seems too subjective to count as a 'miracle,' let me speak of the more visible ones—the ones that altered the trajectory of my life in undeniable ways.

In 1991, I was posted to London—an aspirational assignment that came without lobbying or engineering. Then, in 1994, I was transferred to a challenging post in Srinagar. Within the same year, and against all odds, I was relocated to Mumbai. That transfer became a portal to the miraculous, for it was there—on November 3, 1996—that I found myself organizing the first-ever Music for Meditation and Healing event at Bhabha Atomic Research Centre, Anushaktinagar (described earlier). There was no institutional support, no funds, no prior template—just an inner conviction and the silent force of Sri Swamiji's will. The event happened. And it reverberated not only within me but across the institutional landscape that hosted it.

This was followed by three more such events in Mumbai in 1998, 1999, and 2000—each of them equally improbable in their execution and equally luminous in their impact. What was the miracle here? It was not just that these events occurred but that I, a civil servant with no background in music or event organization, had become the instrument of something much larger.

In 1999, I was selected to lead a team of the Comptroller and Auditor General of India for the audit of the United Nations. A high-level, competitive assignment, it seemed to arrive not just as a reward but as a calling. Soon after, I was transferred to New Delhi—ironically, just as my mother-in-law was diagnosed with breast cancer in Mumbai. She was treated successfully, even as I handled the pressures of a new posting. Once again, it was as though events had rearranged themselves to permit both duty and healing to coexist.

In Delhi, too, the music continued. Not metaphorically, but literally. I had the fortune of organizing four more Music for Meditation and Healing concerts: at FICCI Auditorium, Siri Fort (twice), and Dwarka. Each of these came with its own set of administrative and logistical challenges. Yet each unfolded with precision and grace, and each left behind an audience transformed.

Later, I was once again an instrument in (as I mentioned earlier) organizing the Kumbhabhishekam of Gam Dattanath in Delhi—a deeply moving spiritual milestone. I don't recall ever feeling 'in control' during any of these moments. Rather, I felt 'carried.'

Miracles, Monsoons, and Macaws: Living the Leela of Nāda Brahma

Some miracles crash through the sky with thunder and lightning. Others unfold silently—through impossible logistics, unlikely alignments, and last-minute salvations that no human hand could orchestrate. November 1996 was one such month. And I—then a humble, rather anxious civil servant moonlighting as an amateur event organizer—was right at the heart of it.

The plan had seemed so straightforward, at least on paper. Coordinate and help conduct Music for Meditation and Healing in Mumbai on November 3, 1996. Sri Swamiji had consented. The date was fixed. The venue was secured. But what I lacked was...well, everything else. No local organizational support. No financial cushion. And barely any experience in putting together something of this magnitude. But none of that mattered. I had Sri Swamiji's sankalpa behind me, and somewhere deep inside, I knew that would be enough...

...until nature decided to test my faith.

In the last week of October, just days before the program, a ferocious cyclonic storm struck, lashing coastal Andhra and Karnataka. Floods swept through the region like an angry river god reclaiming forgotten territory. Railway lines between Karnataka and Andhra Pradesh were torn asunder, and the entire network ground to a halt. All trains—all of them—were canceled. And with them, my last thread of hope.

You see, the entire parivar from Mysuru—those who would sing bhajans, offer puja, assist with the havan, and support the healing concert—were all booked to travel by train. Now, they were stranded, with no way to reach Mumbai. As the storm outside raged on, a storm of a different kind began to swirl within me. How was I to explain this to Sri Swamiji?

And then, like a ray of sunlight through a rain-soaked sky, help came from the most unexpected quarters.

Mr B.R. Prabhakara, a senior IAS officer(KN-63) and the then chief secretary to the Government of Karnataka, stepped in. Through the good offices of my boss in the Department of Atomic Energy—Mr C.K. Koshy, himself a respected IAS officer—my desperate appeal found its way to Mr Prabhakara. And he responded—not with hesitation, but with prompt action. A special railway bogie was arranged and tagged onto the only train leaving from Bengaluru toward Mumbai, beating the odds and racing against time. The Mysuru team reached the venue just in time to prepare for the event that would unfold on November 3.

If this wasn't divine choreography, what was?

But the miracles didn't stop there.

Sri Swamiji Himself came and stayed at our home in Mumbai for the duration of the event. We vacated the premises and moved to alternate accommodation so that Sri Swamiji could have complete rest and spiritual space. It wasn't the first time He had graced our home—He had blessed us earlier with visits to London in 1992 and 1993. But to host Him again, now in India, in the very house where I lived and worked and worshipped, was an honor I could scarcely comprehend. Later, He would again stay in our home during His 1999 visit and twice more in Delhi. These weren't just visits; they were sanctifications. To have His lotus feet touch our thresholds was, for us, a karmic reward earned perhaps across many janmas.

Then came the episode of Gam Dattanath Mandir in Swaroopnagar, New Delhi. The approach road to the temple was in shambles—damaged, uneven, and nearly impassable. As preparations for the Kumbhabhishekam of 2004 gathered momentum, I knew the road had to be repaired. I approached the then-municipal commissioner of Delhi, Mr Rakesh Mehta, an IAS officer (75) of the UT cadre. Getting him to bend even slightly from the procedure was like trying to move the Qutub Minar by argument.

But again, with Sri Swamiji's grace flowing through the channels of bureaucratic grit, the impossible began to dissolve. The road was repaired. Not in weeks. Not in months. But in record time.

It was a clear reminder—when it's His will, obstacles turn into opportunities.

And then, the parrots.

Two hyacinth macaws. Rare, radiant, and resplendent in their brilliant blue feathers. A devotee from abroad wished to offer these beautiful birds to Sri Swamiji's Shuka Vana for rehabilitation. But Sri Swamiji, ever a respecter of dharma—not just spiritual, but legal and ecological—refused to accept the donation. 'Get all clearances first,' He insisted. That meant permissions from the Wildlife Department, Customs, and the Environmental Ministry. A bureaucratic trifecta that could normally take months, if not years.

But once again, what happened was nothing short of astonishing. Just one mention of Sri Swamiji's name—just one humble explanation of why the parrots were to be offered—and the barriers fell away like dominoes. Officers who normally spoke in curt memos and red tape now responded with reverence. The papers moved. The permits came through. The parrots arrived.

But the greatest miracle, perhaps, was yet to come.

It wasn't about a storm averted or a road repaired. It wasn't about parrots or programs. It was about people. Hundreds. Thousands. Eventually, millions.

Under the divine baton of Sri Swamiji, mass recitations of the Hanuman Chalisa and the *Bhagavad Gita* were organized by committed and sincere devotees in the USA and India—setting Guinness World Records, yes—but more importantly, setting hearts aflame. These weren't just events of scale. They were events of the soul. Sri Swamiji never allowed us to treat them as spectacles. He would often remind us, 'Don't just chant. Understand. Absorb. Live the meaning.' That was His prescription for true healing—one that cured not just the body but also the intellect and the spirit.

And that is the central truth that keeps playing in my life like a raga that refuses to fade.

When you walk the path with Nāda Brahma, the Universe rearranges itself—storms subside, roads appear, parrots fly in, and people awaken.

All you need to do is surrender and stay tuned. So, were these miracles? To me, yes. Not because the laws of nature were broken but because the flow of life defied probability. These were not random successes. They were orchestrations—symmetries too elegant to be coincidences.

But then comes the difficult question—the philosophical one: if we all die eventually, how is the postponement of death a miracle? To that, I offer this: a miracle is not about beating death. It is about making life count. It is about extending the moment not just in time but in meaning. When Sri Swamiji intervenes, He does not just add days to life—He adds life to days. And what is spiritual strength if not the ability to face mortality with dignity, equanimity, and grace?

This leads me to the final charge: isn't the need for a guru a sign of weakness? My answer is simple. No. The need for a guru is not weakness—it is recognition. Recognition that however intelligent or accomplished we may be, we are not omniscient. That there are forces at work beyond our comprehension. That anchoring in the Divine is not a retreat from strength—it is its source.

Spiritual anchoring doesn't make me superstitious—it makes me grounded. I don't shun science; I embrace it. I don't reject logic; I transcend it when it becomes a wall. The presence of Sri Swamiji in my life has not made me mentally fragile. It has made me inwardly stable. His teachings are not crutches; they are wings.

In the end, life is not a courtroom where faith must defend itself against reason. It is a journey where meaning reveals itself in layers. Some see coincidence, and others see causality. I see grace because through the lens of my life—with all its turns, triumphs, illnesses, and illuminations—I have come to see that miracles are not about spectacle. They are about transformation. The miracle is not that I survived or succeeded—but that I learned to surrender, and in surrender, I discovered the strength I never knew I had. And for that, and for so much more, I owe everything to the living presence of Sri Ganapathy Sachchidananda Swamiji.

References

1. Avadhoota Datta Peetham Official Website.

2. Music for Meditation and Healing.
3. Publications by Devotees.
4. www.study.com-agamas history, significance and texts.
5. www.sreenivasaraos.com-agama shastras and temple worship.
6. www.deccanherald.com-devduttpattanaik/mysterious temple texts called agama.
7. www.studymaster.co.uk-agamas: meaning, definition and examples.
8. https://behindeverytemple.org/temple-science/the-science-of-temple-kumbhabhishekam/
9. www.pluralism.org/kumbhabhishekam
10. www.sribalajis.my.salesforce-sites.com
11. www.svsbalajis.org – mahakumbhbhishekam 2024.

CHAPTER 7

The Eternal Flame – Guru Parampara and the Living Legacy of Sri Ganapathy Sachchidananda Swamiji

Abstract

This chapter explores the sacred tradition of Guru Parampara, the unbroken lineage of spiritual masters in the Datta tradition, with a special focus on the life and mission of Sri Ganapathy Sachchidananda Swamiji. Beginning with a deep dive into the philosophical meaning of the word 'Guru' as described in Guru Gita, it then traces the origins of the Datta lineage to Bhagawan Dattatreya, the primordial Guru who is the embodiment of the Trimurti—Brahma, Vishnu, and Shiva. The chapter journeys through the illustrious incarnations of Sripada Sri Vallabha and Sri Narasimha Saraswati, revealing their profound influence on Indian spirituality. This spiritual river ultimately flows into the modern era, culminating in the luminous presence of Sri Swamiji. His life, from a miraculous birth on a rock in the Kaveri River to the establishment of Avadhoota Datta Peetham in Mysuru, is portrayed not just as a continuation of the Datta tradition but as its living embodiment. Through His teachings, music, healing work, and global outreach, Sri Swamiji exemplifies the true purpose of a guru: to dispel darkness, awaken divine knowledge, and guide seekers toward liberation.

The tradition of Guru Parampara is a glowing stream of divine wisdom flowing through time, unbroken and uninterrupted, from one enlightened master to another. The very term Guru Parampara combines two Sanskrit words—guru, the dispeller of darkness, and parampara, the sacred succession. As revealed in the ancient scripture *Guru Gita*, a conversation between Lord Shiva and Goddess Parvati, 'gu' stands for darkness and 'ru' for the light that removes it. Thus, the guru is no mere teacher but the sun of knowledge who annihilates the shadows of ignorance, illuminating the seeker's path with divine insight. The guru is exalted in every scripture as the embodiment of pure, spiritual wisdom—Gnaana itself.

In the Indian spiritual tradition, no seeker can traverse the inner terrain without the guiding presence of a guru. It is not merely a custom to worship the guru lineage; it is the seeker's sacred duty, for the guru is unparalleled. No one can equal His stature, and no worship is greater than worship to Him. Without the blessings of a guru, the ultimate goal of self-realization remains a distant dream. That is why, in every ritual, every undertaking—spiritual or worldly—the guru must be worshipped before and after. Through this offering of gratitude to the luminous lineage, the seeker draws closer to the Supreme knowledge.

To truly ascend the ladder of spiritual evolution, one must find a living guru—a physical embodiment of divinity. Serving such a guru with love, reverence, and unwavering faith becomes the path to inner purification. When the mind is cleansed of its restlessness, sins, and impurities, the Atman—the true Self—reveals itself, shimmering in the silence of self-realization. *Guru Gita* affirms this truth in mystical poetry, stating that the guru is beyond all attributes (gunas) and form (roopa), a direct manifestation of the formless Supreme reality.

In this exalted line of gurus stands Sri Ganapathy Sachchidananda Swamiji, a radiant jewel in the crown of the Datta Guru Parampara. But before we arrive at Him, we must journey back to the primordial source of this tradition: Bhagawan Dattatreya, the eternal Guru of gurus.

Bhagawan Dattatreya is no ordinary deity—He is the very embodiment of the cosmic Trinity: Brahma—the creator; Vishnu—the sustainer; and Shiva—the destroyer, all united in a single divine form. Born to the sage Atri and the supremely virtuous Anasuya in the mysterious and mystical epoch of Kriya Yuga, Datta descended as the answer to intense austerity and divine will. He did not come to preach doctrine or dogma—He came to walk among seekers, to uplift them, and to reveal the spiritual truth through the silent power of presence.

One of the most captivating legends of Datta is His teaching to King Yadu, where He reveals that His gurus were not just holy men but the entire universe itself. From the earth, He learned patience, from water purity, from the sky detachment. From birds and beasts, insects, and natural elements, He gleaned profound spiritual truths. His life became the ultimate teaching—that the Divine is everywhere, and every moment is a lesson in self-realization.

As time flowed into the darkening age of Kali Yuga, humanity began to lose its ability to perceive the divine directly. People became sluggish in spirit, tethered to material pursuits, and the radiant form of Bhagawan Datta became invisible to their eyes. But compassion was His nature, and He never abandoned His children. Whenever the world needed a spiritual light, He returned in physical form to uplift, guide, and purify. Among these incarnations, Sripada Vallabha and Narasimha Saraswati stand tall as timeless spiritual beacons.

Sripada Sri Vallabha, the first incarnation of Datta in Kali Yuga, was born in the holy town of Pithapuram in Andhra Pradesh. The child bore the Divine marks of Shankha and Chakra on his feet and was recognized early on as a divine personality.

Renouncing worldly life at a young age, Sripada embarked on a pilgrimage across India—Kashi, Badrinath, Gokarna, and finally, Kuruvapur, where He performed innumerable miracles and imparted spiritual teachings to all who came to Him. His compassion knew no bounds; His words pierced illusion, and His presence dissolved bondage. It was He who promised a grieving mother that He would be born as her son in the next birth—thus paving the way for His next incarnation.

Sri Narasimha Saraswati, the second Datta incarnation, was born in the village of Karanja in Maharashtra to a devout Brahmin couple. From early childhood, signs of divinity sparkled in his eyes. He renounced the world as a boy and set out to awaken the slumbering hearts of humanity. Through yogic miracles and profound teachings, He inspired kings and commoners alike. Even a Muslim ruler who came to test Him became His devotee. He traveled far and wide, sowing the seeds of spiritual wisdom and showing the path of inner transformation.

This unbroken lineage of the Guru Parampara, glowing like a garland of stars, ultimately flows into the present age, culminating in the living, breathing presence of Sri Ganapathy Sachchidananda Swamiji. Revered as the Avadhoota Datta Peethadhipati, He is the modern torchbearer of this eternal spiritual flame.

Born, as mentioned earlier, on a rock in the sacred Kaveri River at Mekedatu, Karnataka, Sri Swamiji's arrival was foreseen by a Hindu saint and a Moslem Fakir who told His parents, Sri Narasimha Sastry and Sri Jayalakshmi Mata, that the child would uplift the world with divine knowledge. At birth, the child was covered in holy ash—a sign of his Avadhoota nature. Named Satyanarayana, He was trained in spiritual disciplines by His mother, whom He lovingly calls His first guru.

From his early years, Sri Swamiji displayed miraculous powers, oceanic compassion, and an uncanny understanding of people's past, present, and future. He wandered like a mystic monk, singing soul-stirring bhajans on riverbanks, organizing satsangs in village huts, and healing people through His mere presence. Gradually, disciples gathered around Him, drawn by His divine magnetism.

In 1966, the small flame of His mission took root in Mysuru, where He established the Avadhoota Datta Peetham—today a sprawling spiritual citadel of Vedic tradition, healing music, and humanitarian service. Sri Swamiji has become a global ambassador (described earlier) of Nāda Chikitsa (Music Therapy), performing healing ragas across the world, from the Royal Albert Hall in London to the Sydney Opera House. He continues the mission of Datta—not just by teachings but by transformation. People come to Him for solace, clarity, healing, and inner elevation.

The Datta Peetham's Guru Parampara Prayer beautifully captures this divine lineage. It begins with salutations to Sri Ganapathy, the remover of obstacles, and to Saraswati, the goddess of wisdom. It then flows into invocations to Sripada Vallabha and Narasimha Saraswati—the majestic pillars of the Datta tradition—and culminates in the living presence of Sri Swamiji, the ever-present guru.

To be in this tradition is to be in the flow of a mighty river of wisdom and compassion. The guru is the bridge from the temporal to the eternal, from bondage to liberation. Sri Ganapathy Sachchidananda Swamiji does not merely preach this truth—He is that bridge. In His eyes is the timeless gaze of Dattatreya, in His voice the healing nectar of divine song, and in His life the living testament of Guru Parampara itself.

The Guru Parampara is not a mere concept of lineage—it is a sacred lifeline that carries the torch of enlightenment from one generation to the next, from ancient sages to modern saints. In the Datta tradition, this lineage takes on a special dimension, for it is anchored in the infinite consciousness of Bhagawan Dattatreya, the Guru of gurus. Through His incarnations, He adapts to the changing times, guiding humanity in forms suited to their spiritual needs. In this age, Sri Ganapathy Sachchidananda Swamiji stands as that guiding light—effulgent, compassionate, and transformative. His birth, life, teachings, and tireless work are not just a continuation of the Guru Parampara; they are its flowering in full glory. Through Sri Swamiji, the ancient truths have found a modern voice, and the eternal river of wisdom has found a new course to flow. For seekers of this age and those to come, His presence is not merely inspirational—it is indispensable. In the heart of Sri Swamiji, the flame of the Datta tradition burns bright, lighting the path for countless souls toward divine realization.

References

1. Avadhoota Datta Peetham. (n.d.). Sri Ganapathy Sachchidananda Swamiji – Life and Mission. Retrieved from https://www.dattapeetham.org

2. Avadhoota Datta Peetham. (n.d.). Guru Parampara and Datta Lineage. Retrieved from https://www.dattapeetham.org/page/view/sri-ganapathy-sachchidananda-swamiji

3. Avadhoota Datta Peetham. (n.d.). Guru Parampara Prayer. Mysuru: Sri Ganapathy Sachchidananda Ashrama Publications.

4. Avadhoota Datta Peetham. (n.d.). Nāda Chikitsa – Music for Meditation and Healing. Retrieved from https://www.dattapeetham.org/page/view/bhajans-and-healing-music

5. Dattatreya, Lord. (n.d.). Teachings to King Yadu – 24 Gurus of Nature. As recorded in *Srimad Bhagavatam*, Canto 11, Chapter 7.

6. Ganapathy Sachchidananda Swamiji. (2005). *Guru Gita*: With Commentary by Sri Swamiji. Mysuru: SGS Ashrama Publications.

7. Ganapathy Sachchidananda Swamiji. (n.d.). *Sripada Srivallabha Charitamrutam* (English translation). Retrieved from https://www.sripadavallabha.org

8. Kaleshwar, S (2004). *Shirdi Sai Baba: The Universal Master*. Penukonda: Soul University Press. (Contains reference to Guru lineage and Datta tradition.)

9. Sundar, A (2012). Avadhoota Datta Peetham: A Modern Spiritual Institution. In Contemporary Hindu Spirituality (pp. 157–175). Delhi: Bharatiya Vidya Bhavan.

10. Swami, MP (2000). *Sri Guru Charitra: Life of Narasimha Saraswati*. (Translated from Marathi). Hyderabad: Datta Mahasamsthanam Publications.

CHAPTER 8

Breath of the Divine: The Transformative Power of Datta Kriya Yoga

Abstract

This chapter presents an in-depth exploration of Datta Kriya Yoga, a unique system of yogic breathing and meditation developed and taught by Pujya Sri Ganapathy Sachchidananda Swamiji. Rooted in the ancient yogic wisdom of Bhagawan Dattatreya, the primordial guru, this holistic practice integrates elements of Ashtanga Yoga,[47]

47. Ashtanga Yoga (अष्टाङ्गयोग) means the 'Eight-Limbed Path' of yoga, outlined by Sage Patanjali in the Yoga Sūtras. It offers a comprehensive system for attaining self-discipline, inner peace, and ultimately, liberation (moksha). The eight limbs are: Yama – Ethical restraints (e.g., non-violence, truth), Niyama – Personal disciplines (e.g., purity, contentment), Asana – Physical postures for stability and health, Praṇayama – Control of breath and life energy, Pratyahara – Withdrawal of senses from external objects, Dharana – Concentration on a single point or object, Dhyana – Meditation or uninterrupted flow of awareness, Samadhi – Complete absorption or union with the Divine. Together, these limbs form a holistic path from external discipline to inner realization.

Hatha Yoga,[48] *Kundalini Yoga,*[49] *and Raja Yoga*[50] *into a single, accessible method suitable for all. Accredited by the Ministry of AYUSH, Government of India, Datta Kriya Yoga offers a scientific and spiritual approach to health and inner transformation. Through the cultivation of conscious breath and the subtle movement of pranic energy, practitioners awaken vitality, deepen self-awareness, and align with the universal force of life. The chapter also explores the yogic legacy of Sri Jayalakshmi Mata, the spiritual force behind Sri Swamiji's mastery, and discusses how Datta Kriya Yoga contributes to modern well-being by offering immunity support, emotional balance, stress relief, and spiritual growth—thus affirming its role not just as a health regimen but as a path to inner bliss and human unity.*

---

48. Haṭha Yoga is a traditional branch of yoga that emphasizes physical discipline as a means to prepare the body and mind for spiritual awakening. 'Ha' means sun (active energy), 'tha' means moon (passive energy), symbolizing the balance of opposing forces within us. It includes asanas (yogic postures) for strength and flexibility, praṇayama (breath control) to regulate life force, mudras and bandhas (gestures and locks) to channel energy, shatkriyas (cleansing techniques) for detoxification. It leads ultimately to dhyana (meditation) and samadhi (absorption). Haṭha Yoga serves as the foundation for many modern yoga styles and is a key step toward mastering the higher limbs of Raja Yoga.

49. Kundalini Yoga is a spiritual practice focused on awakening the Kundalini Shakti—a dormant spiritual energy believed to reside at the base of the spine. Through a combination of praṇayama (breath control), asanas (postures), mantra chanting, mudras (hand gestures), dhyana (meditation), the energy is gradually activated and guided upward through the chakras, leading to expanded awareness, inner transformation, and ultimately, union with the Divine (samadhi). Kundalini Yoga is both powerful and transformative and is traditionally taught under the guidance of a realized guru, as it involves intense energetic shifts.

50. Raja Yoga is the 'royal path' of yoga that emphasizes mastery over the mind through meditation and inner control. It is based on the Yoga Sūtras of Patanjali and incorporates the eightfold path (Ashtanga Yoga). Raja Yoga aims to still the mind (*chitta vritti nirodha*) and realize the **Self (Atman)**. It is considered the **path of mental and spiritual kingship**, leading to inner freedom and enlightenment.

~

Datta Kriya Yoga is more than a system of exercises—it is a profound spiritual technology developed for the modern world. At its heart lies the ancient truth: life is measured not in years but in breaths. The slower and deeper one breathes, the longer and more consciously one lives. This principle, known to ancient yogis for millennia, now finds scientific backing, and it is this very insight that forms the cornerstone of Datta Kriya Yoga.

Sri Ganapathy Sachchidananda Swamiji, the living torchbearer of the Dattatreya tradition, has revived and refined this sacred science for today's humanity. Through decades of experiential wisdom and divine guidance, Sri Swamiji has created a comprehensive yet simple practice that brings balance to our fragmented lives. This system, called Datta Kriya Yoga, has now received official recognition as a certified 'Yoga Training Center' by the Yoga Certification Board under the Ministry of AYUSH, Government of India—a testament to its authenticity, effectiveness, and global relevance.

The practice itself is deeply rooted in the breath. Pranayama—the art of conscious breathing—takes center stage. Practitioners are taught to regulate inhalation, exhalation, and breath retention with awareness and precision. Each pranayama session is followed by a specific kriya—a subtle energy movement that purifies the mind and settles the nervous system. Mudras—yogic gestures—are used to redirect pranic energy to various parts of the body, enhancing immunity, digestion, circulation, and even emotional well-being. These techniques, when practiced consistently, cleanse the nadis (energy channels), awaken dormant energy, and slowly guide the practitioner to a deeper awareness of the self.

The brilliance of Datta Kriya Yoga lies in its accessibility. It is designed to suit people from all walks of life, regardless of age, fitness level, or background. Whether one is a busy professional, a student, or a retiree, the methods can be adapted to any schedule and physical condition. It is non-sectarian, inclusive, and respects all spiritual paths, functioning as a universal bridge that connects body, mind, and spirit.

What distinguishes this system even more is its deeply personal lineage. Sri Swamiji's understanding of Kundalini and pranic energy is not merely theoretical—it is a living, breathing realization inherited from his own Guru and mother, Sri Jayalakshmi Mata. A master of Sri Vidya and Raja Yoga, she was the force behind his spiritual awakening, transferring her energy to him through Shaktipat.[51] This descent of energy shaped Sri Swamiji's yogic journey and allowed him to design a method that merges the subtle with the practical. In every breath, every movement of Datta Kriya Yoga, one can sense the play of her divine inspiration and Sri Swamiji's boundless compassion.

The components of the practice are thoughtfully structured. It begins with Nadi Shuddhi Vyayama[52]—subtle yogic movements to prepare the body and clear the energy pathways. This is followed by asanas (postures) to tone the muscles and

51. Shaktipat is the spiritual transmission of divine energy or awakening power from a guru to a disciple, often through touch, gaze, word, or mere intention. This awakening activates the dormant kundalini energy within the seeker, initiating a deep inner transformation and accelerated spiritual progress.

52. Naḍī Shuddhi Vyayama is a yogic practice focused on purifying the energy channels (naḍīs) in the subtle body through specific breathing exercises and gentle movements. 'Naḍī' refers to the praṇic pathways through which life force (praṇa) flows. 'Shuddhi' means purification. 'Vyayama' means exercise or movement. The practice typically includes alternate nostril breathing (Naḍī Shavadhuta gitaodhana Praṇayama), simple stretching and twisting movements coordinated with the breath, and focused awareness to cleanse and balance Ida, Piṅgala, and Suṣumna naḍīs. Naḍī Shuddhi Vyayama helps remove energetic blockages, enhances vitality, calms the mind, and prepares the body for deeper yogic practices like meditation and Kundalini awakening.

open the body, and then pranayama to bring the breath into a conscious rhythm. Mudras are introduced to fine-tune the pranic flow. The practice culminates in dhyana—meditation, where the inner silence deepens, and the seeker meets the still center within.

The benefits are wide-ranging and profound. Physical strength and flexibility improve, chronic ailments like blood pressure and diabetes stabilize, and stress levels drop. At a subtler level, the mind becomes clearer, the focus sharpens, and the will strengthens. Most importantly, there is a growing inner joy—unshaken by circumstances and radiant from within. In a world overrun by anxiety, disconnection, and imbalance, Datta Kriya Yoga offers not just a remedy but a revolution—one breath at a time.

Over the years, Sri Swamiji has conducted workshops, retreats, and training sessions across continents, bringing this gift to schools, corporate offices, medical institutions, and spiritual gatherings. Whether in India or abroad, the message remains the same: breath is life, and conscious breath is divine life. When harnessed with the tools of Datta Kriya Yoga, the breath becomes the bridge between suffering and serenity, chaos and clarity, fragmentation and wholeness.

What makes this even more significant is Sri Swamiji's vision behind the practice. Datta Kriya Yoga is not just about personal well-being—it is a call to unity in diversity. By calming the breath and aligning the mind, the individual naturally becomes more harmonious, more peaceful, and more attuned to the collective human experience. This inner transformation radiates outward, bringing healing to families, communities, and, ultimately, the planet.

Yoga, as Sri Swamiji often reminds us, does not end with fitness. It begins there. True yoga gives us mastery over the mind, not just flexibility in the body. It offers a way—not just to manage life but to transcend it. Though there may be many spiritual paths, all of them require the guidance of a pure mind, and for that, Yoga is essential. Datta Kriya Yoga offers this essential key in a language that is both ancient and urgently modern.

Datta Kriya Yoga is a living tradition that bridges breath and being, body and soul, science and spirit. Rooted in the sacred wisdom of Bhagawan Dattatreya and brought to life by the realized presence of Sri Ganapathy Sachchidananda Swamiji, it offers a beacon of health, healing, and inner harmony in a world spinning ever faster. Its power lies not only in its techniques but in the presence of the master who embodies it. Through His vision, compassion, and divine experience, Sri Swamiji has made Datta Kriya Yoga a tool for global transformation—accessible, inclusive, and profoundly uplifting. For those who seek not just health but wholeness, not just peace but purpose, Datta Kriya Yoga is a sacred answer drawn from the breath of the Divine.

One question that may arise in the minds of readers who may not be well versed in different systems and forms of yoga is how exactly the systems of yoga are different from each other in terms of objectives, theory, and practice. While I do not claim expertise in these systems, my detailed inquiries with the acclaimed practitioners of various forms of yoga over the years led me to formulate a comparison. This will be discussed in the next chapter.

References

1. Avadhoota Datta Peetham. (n.d.). *Datta Kriya Yoga: A Breath-Based Yoga Program for Health and Healing*. Mysuru, India: Avadhoota Datta Peetham Publications. Retrieved from https://www.dattapeetham.org

2. Avadhoota Datta Peetham. (n.d.). *Healing Music* (Nāda Chikitsa). Retrieved from https://www.dattapeetham.org/page/view/bhajans-and-healing-music

3. Avadhoota Datta Peetham. (n.d.). *Sri Jayalakshmi Mata – The Divine Mother.* Retrieved from https://www.dattapeetham.org/page/view/jayalakshmi-mata

4. Avadhoota Datta Peetham. (n.d.). *Datta Kriya Yoga Accreditation and Workshops.* Retrieved from https://www.dattapeetham.org/page/view/datta-kriya-yoga

5. Ganapathy Sachchidananda Swamiji. (n.d.). *Nāda Chikitsa: Healing Through Sound. Discourses and performances.* Mysuru: Sri Ganapathy Sachchidananda Ashrama Archives.

6. Ministry of AYUSH, Government of India. (n.d.). *List of Recognized Yoga Training Centres.* Yoga Certification Board. Retrieved from https://yogacertificationboard.nic.in

7. Sundar, A (2012). *Avadhoota Datta Peetham: A Modern Spiritual Institution.* In Contemporary Hindu Spirituality (pp. 157–175). Delhi: Bharatiya Vidya Bhavan.

8. Swamiji, SGS (2006). *Raja Yoga: A Spiritual Journey Within.* Mysuru, India: Datta Publications.

CHAPTER 9

Breath, Balance, and Beyond: A Comparative Insight into Modern Yogic Systems

Abstract

This chapter explores the unique characteristics of Datta Kriya Yoga as taught by Sri Ganapathy Sachchidananda Swamiji, comparing it with other prominent yoga systems propagated by renowned spiritual leaders such as Paramahansa Yogananda, Jaggi Vasudev (Sadhguru), Sri Sri Ravi Shankar, and Baba Ramdev. While all these systems aim to promote physical health, emotional balance, and spiritual awareness through breath control and meditation, they differ in their source traditions, techniques, and emphasis. Datta Kriya Yoga distinguishes itself through its integration of breath control, sound healing (Nāda Chikitsa), and devotion to Bhagawan Dattatreya, offering a holistic approach to spiritual evolution.

One of the questions that any seeker of yoga is confronted with is multiple systems, names, and approaches to yoga. Each is as efficient as the other and has staunch followers and practitioners. The Guru of Yogashastra, Patanjali, is the source or origin of all forms of yoga that are in vogue. In this chapter, I have tried to attempt a simple enough comparison of the more prevalent yoga practices in the country with the method of Yoga that Sri Ganapathy Sachchidananda Swamiji has been propagating.

Datta Kriya Yoga is unique in both approach and intent, differing from the systems taught by other contemporary or acclaimed past masters like Swami Yogananda Paramahansa, Jaggi Vasudev (Sadhguru), Sri Sri Ravi Shankar, and Baba Ramdev. While all of them promote physical health, emotional balance, and spiritual awareness through breath and meditation, the source traditions, techniques, and emphasis would appear quite distinct.

Here's how Sri Swamiji's Kriya Yoga could, in my opinion—and as gathered from experts exposed to these systems of yoga—compare with the systems of yoga propagated by other illustrious spiritual masters. This is my personal view.

A. Compared to Swami Yogananda Paramhamsa's Kriya Yoga

Kriya Yoga, as taught by Paramahamsa Yogananda, and Datta Kriya Yoga, as taught by Sri Ganapathy Sachchidananda Swamiji, are both profound systems of spiritual discipline rooted in Sanatana Dharma[53] and aim to harmonize the body, mind, and breath to awaken inner divinity. While both share the term 'Kriya Yoga' and draw from ancient yogic traditions,

53. Sanātana Dharma, meaning "eternal law" or "eternal order" is the original Sanskrit term for what is now commonly known as Hinduism, encompassing the timeless spiritual truths and ethical principles that govern the universe. It emphasizes dharma (righteous living), karma (action and consequence), and moksha (liberation), guiding adherents toward harmony with cosmic order and ultimate self-realization.

they differ in methodology, emphasis, transmission, and philosophical framing. Kriya Yoga, as revived and popularized in the modern era by Paramahamsa Yogananda (author of *Autobiography of a Yogi*), is based on a lineage passed down from Mahavatar Babaji,[54] Lahiri Mahasaya, Sri Yukteswar, and ultimately to Swami Yogananda himself. The system integrates ancient pranayama with deep meditation, rooted in Raja Yoga as outlined in Patanjali's Yoga Sutras.

The essential aspects include

i. **Kriya Pranayama:** A powerful technique of energy control, where the practitioner mentally guides life energy (prana) up and down the spinal axis (sushumna), from the muladhara to the sahasrara, synchronized with the breath. This internal 'breathless' circulation is said to accelerate spiritual evolution.

ii. **Hong-Sau and Om Techniques:** Preliminary meditation techniques used to still the mind and interiorize awareness. 'Hong-Sau' is used to watch the natural breath, and the 'Om Technique' involves auditory meditation on the cosmic vibration.

iii. **Devotion (Bhakti)**: Deep emphasis is placed on the loving relationship between the soul and God. Yogananda considered devotion to be the most powerful tool on the spiritual path.

iv. **Guru Parampara:** The method is received through initiation and authorized instruction from a recognized teacher within the lineage. The guru-disciple relationship is central.

---

54. Mahavatar Babaji is a legendary immortal yogi believed to have maintained a physical body for centuries, guiding advanced spiritual seekers and reviving Kriya Yoga for the modern age. Revered in the lineage of Lahiri Mahasaya and popularized by Paramahansa Yogananda in *Autobiography of a Yogi*, Babaji is said to appear only to a few chosen disciples, radiating divine presence and timeless wisdom.

v. **Inner Realization:** Kriya Yoga is not just physical or energetic; it aims to bring the practitioner into direct experience of the soul's unity with God through deep interiorization.

Essentials of Sri Ganapathy Sachchidananda Swamiji's Datta Kriya Yoga

Datta Kriya Yoga, taught by Sri Ganapathy Sachchidananda Swamiji, is a synthesis of breath control (pranayama), subtle awareness, sound (nāda), and meditative stillness, deeply infused with devotion to Bhagawan Dattatreya, the Adi Guru. It is designed for both beginners and advanced practitioners, with health and spiritual evolution as dual goals.

The core components are:

i. **Conscious Breathing (Kriya Pranayama):** A sequence of regulated breathing techniques to balance the pancha pranas, calm the mind, and regulate the nervous system. These include deep breathing, alternate nostril breathing (nadi shodhana), and rhythmic inhalation-exhalation cycles.

ii. **Sound and Healing (Nāda Chikitsa):** Use of mantras, musical notes (ragas), and internal awareness of sound vibrations. Swamiji integrates his Music for Meditation and Healing as part of the yogic process.

iii. **Mudras and Bandhas:** Certain gestures and internal locks are employed to retain and circulate energy in the body.

iv. **Datta Consciousness:** The focus is not only on energy but on divine awareness, particularly the connection to Lord Dattatreya, seen as the embodiment of the Guru Principle and the triple aspect of divinity (Brahma-Vishnu-Shiva).

v. **Accessibility and Health Benefits:** Datta Kriya Yoga is designed to be inclusive, so even beginners can benefit. While it leads to higher states of meditation, it also emphasizes physical healing, stress relief, and emotional purification.

vi. **Adaptability:** Sri Swamiji has structured Datta Kriya Yoga with flexibility for modern life, offering guided sessions, mobile apps, and tools for gradual progression without the requirement of formal initiation.

In essence, Swami Yogananda's Kriya Yoga stems from the Mahavatar Babaji lineage via Lahiri Mahasaya. It emphasizes pranayama and inner awareness practices aimed at awakening Kundalini in a highly structured, secretive, initiation-based format. Sri Swamiji's Datta Kriya Yoga is less rigid, more accessible, and not esoteric. It does not require secret initiation. While Kundalini's awakening is acknowledged, the emphasis is on breath purification, energy flow (prana), and emotional healing. It is deeply rooted in the Dattatreya tradition and His own experiential lineage via Sri Jayalakshmi Mata, not Babaji.

B. Compared to Isha Yoga (Shri Jaggi Vasudev)

• **Isha Yoga Focus:** Sadhguru's system is structured around Inner Engineering, combining kriyas (like Shambhavi Mahamudra), meditative awareness, and Hatha Yoga, aiming to bring balance and clarity for worldly functioning and spiritual evolution. It leans toward non-dual awareness (Shiva-based).

• **Sri Swamiji's Difference:** Datta Kriya Yoga is more aligned with Vedantic, devotional, and Raja Yoga principles. It integrates sound therapy (Nāda Chikitsa) and devotional elements along with yogic breathwork. Unlike Isha's non-theistic tone, Sri Swamiji's yoga flows from a living guru-disciple dynamic and draws on Bhakti (devotion) as well as yoga.

C. Compared to Sudarshana Kriya (Sri Ravi Shankar)

• **Sudarshana Kriya:** A rhythmic breathing technique taught en masse for stress relief, emotional cleansing, and mental clarity. It follows a specific, timed cyclic breathing pattern and is widely taught in structured workshops.

• **Sri Swamiji's Difference:** Datta Kriya Yoga goes beyond rhythmic breathwork. It includes subtle energy movement (kriyas), mudras, asanas, pranayama, and meditation, adapted to individual needs. It is less standardized, more therapeutic, and deeply spiritual in tone, often guided in person by Sri Swamiji or trained disciples.

D. Compared to Baba Ramdev's Yoga

• **Baba Ramdev's Focus:** Primarily a public health and wellness approach using accessible asanas, pranayamas like Kapalabhati and Anulom-Vilom, and Ayurveda. It emphasizes curing physical ailments and popularizing yoga among the masses.

• **Sri Swamiji's Difference:** Datta Kriya Yoga is not just for physical health—it is a spiritual sadhana integrating breath, meditation, sound healing (Nāda), and devotion. It does have health benefits but aims at inner purification, subtle body activation, and spiritual elevation, rooted in Kundalini and Raja Yoga, not mass fitness alone.

Each of the yoga systems and variants has its own appeal and set of serious and devoted practitioners who have benefitted immensely therefrom. In summary, and as I understand, Datta Kriya Yoga is a subtle, spiritually charged, devotional, breath-and-prana-based system, grounded in the Guru Parampara of Bhagawan Dattatreya and distinct for its integration of nāda (sound) and energy work. It is customizable, experiential, and non-dogmatic, intended not just for health but for awakening the deeper consciousness and aligning the body-mind-spirit complex in harmony with divine presence.

Datta Kriya Yoga, as taught by Sri Ganapathy Sachchidananda Swamiji, offers a distinctive and holistic approach to spiritual practice. Its integration of breath control, sound healing, and devotion sets it apart from other yoga systems, providing practitioners with a comprehensive path to physical well-being, emotional balance, and spiritual awakening. By comparing Datta Kriya Yoga with other prominent practices, we gain a deeper understanding of the diverse methodologies available, allowing individuals to choose a path that resonates most profoundly with their personal spiritual goals.

Let me now come, in the next chapter, to another dimension of Sri Swamiji's personality, which is His powerful musical compositions or bhajans. Each of the bhajans or keertanas has embedded powerful beejaakshara (seed letter), carries the name of the tune or raga, and invokes/evokes a crucial aspect of divinity. These bhajans have been used by Sri Swamiji in His Music for Meditation and Healing events across the world.

References

1. Datta Kriya Yoga. (n.d.). Retrieved from www.dattapeetham.org.
2. Kriya Yoga Path of Meditation - Self Realization Fellowship. (n.d.). Retrieved from https://yogananda.org/kriya-yoga-path-of-meditation.
3. Datta Kriya Yoga - Avadhoota Datta Peetham. (n.d.). Retrieved from www.dattapeetham.org
4. Datta Kriya Yoga - Jesus Datta Retreat Center. (n.d.). Retrieved from https://www.dattaretreatcenter.org
5. Datta Kriya Yoga on the App Store - Apple. (n.d.).
6. https://isha.sadhguru.org/en/wisdom/video/yoga-for-inner-exploration-shambhavi-mudra?utm_source
7. https://patanjaliwellness.com
8. https://www.artofliving.org/in-en/about-us/sudarshan-kriya

CHAPTER 10

Sacred Soundscapes: The Transformative Bhajans of Sri Ganapathy Sachchidananda Swamiji

Abstract

This chapter delves into the profound spiritual, philosophical, and musical dimensions of select bhajan compositions by Sri Ganapathy Sachchidananda Swamiji, who has composed over 3,000 keerthanas across various languages. Through an in-depth analysis of key compositions—such as 'Manasa Mandira,' 'Rama Hare Jaya Saure,' 'Disi Disi Sam Vasasi Vibho,' 'Jaya Bhagavati Lalite,' and 'Kanakaligaya Vedalingaya Vai Namaha'—the chapter explores how Sri Swamiji seamlessly blends poetic elegance, classical ragas, and devotional intensity to create sacred experiences. Each composition is examined for its lyrical meaning, raga-based emotional resonance, and spiritual objective. The section further expands to a second level of analysis, highlighting eight masterpieces that reflect core themes in Hindu spirituality: surrender, purification, non-duality, divine motherhood, union of Shiva and Shakti, inner realization, and mantra yoga. Rich with philosophical insights and esoteric symbolism, these bhajans are shown to be vehicles of Nāda Chikitsa—healing through sound—and serve as portals to inner awakening. The compositions are aligned with both classical grammar and yogic purpose, showcasing Sri Swamiji's unparalleled ability to marry the structure of music with the flow of spiritual grace.

The bhajan compositions (as stated earlier, there are more than 3,000 and in different languages) of Pujya Sri Ganapathy Sachchidananda Swamiji form a vast ocean of sacred sound, where each ripple and wave bears a unique flavor of devotion, beauty, and spiritual insight. Unless one selects specific compositions, one would not appreciate the uniqueness of the lyrics, raga, or tune and the composite purpose or objective. How to select a few among 3,000 compositions?

I graciously acknowledge the inputs and suggestions I received from my elder son Anirudh, who is an avid music enthusiast and a serious practitioner of violin. He is deeply interested in understanding various nuances of Carnatic music and is an 'out and out' admirer of the superlative attributes of the compositions of Sri Swamiji for a long time. It is he who provided hitherto unknown insights (definitely to me) about the combination of depth, significance of tunes, lyrical value, and philosophical profoundness of the compositions of Sri Swamiji. He guided me in exploring some of the dimensions of the compositions of Sri Swamiji through various unexpected but available sources, including AI and the Internet. The latter is a veritable storehouse of great analytical data and material on the compositions of Sri Swamiji, which I used and acknowledged in the chapter.

I attempt to choose the following five bhajans—'Manasa Mandira,' 'Rama Hare Jaya Saure,' 'Disi Disi Sam Vasasi Vibho,' 'Jaya Bhagawati Lalite,' and 'Kanakaligaya Vedalingaya Vai Namaha'—which are acknowledged as some of the most luminous jewels in this ocean. These exemplify Sri Swamiji's unparalleled ability to synthesize poetic elegance with precise musical architecture and philosophical clarity. Each composition, while distinct in its tone and emotional tenor, shares the common thread of Nāda Brahma—the Divine as sound—and reveals how carefully Sri Swamiji selects ragas and rhythms not only to please the ear but to elevate the soul.

'Manasa Mandira' is a contemplative and inward-facing bhajan. Literally translating to 'Temple of the Mind,' the song is an invocation for the purification and sanctification of the inner self. Lyrically, it draws on the metaphor of the human mind as a temple where the Divine resides. The composition is simple, elegant, and meditative, making use of gentle, flowing meter and direct imagery. Sri Swamiji's literary craftsmanship shines in the seamless union of internal and external sanctity—urging the devotee to decorate not just physical shrines but the mental altar with purity, sincerity, and stillness. Musically, this bhajan is often rendered in Raga Kapi or Raga Desh, both of which are known for their softness and emotional depth. These ragas carry a tone of affectionate yearning and bhakti—fitting for a piece that calls the listener to cleanse the mind through introspection and devotion. The slow, unhurried tempo allows each syllable to sink in deeply, making the bhajan a powerful aid for dhyana (meditation).

In contrast, 'Rama Hare Jaya Saure' is a vibrant, almost jubilant chant that glorifies multiple forms of the Divine, including Rama and Vishnu in His form as Hari and Sauri (a name of Krishna). The bhajan is built on a repetitive refrain, a hallmark of kirtan-style singing, which allows both individual and group participation to flourish. Lyrically, it fuses two great traditions—Rama bhakti and Krishna bhakti—uniting them in one breath. There is both reverence and rhythm, praise and playful melody. The composition often rides the energy of Raga Hamsadhwani or Raga Mohanam, two pentatonic ragas known for their auspicious and uplifting quality. These ragas are especially effective in evoking joy, clarity, and divine enthusiasm. The bhajan is usually set to a fast-paced rhythm (e.g., Adi Tala), invoking a state of spiritual excitement that energizes the listener while keeping them grounded in devotion. The choice of tune reflects Sri Swamiji's keen sensitivity to audience reception—here, he offers a musical doorway that is both simple and powerful, accessible to all regardless of classical training.

The third bhajan, 'Disi Disi Sam Vasasi Vibho,' reveals the cosmic expanse of the Divine. The very phrase 'disi disi' (in all directions) emphasizes the all-pervading presence of the Supreme being. Lyrically, this composition is rich with Sanskritized diction and poetic grandeur. The use of 'Vibho,' 'Isha,' 'Adhokshaja,' and other Vedantic terms shows the depth of scriptural knowledge embedded in Swamiji's bhajan literature. This is not only a song of praise but also of realization—an assertion of the Vedic truth that the Self, the Brahman, is everywhere. The melody selected is usually one of the more meditative or devotional ragas, such as Raga Shubhapantuvarali or Raga Charukesi, which allow a fusion of majesty and compassion to flow simultaneously. The bhajan structure moves like a stotra but with the melodic sensitivity of a prayer—inviting the devotee to merge their perception with the formless, all-encompassing Divine. The depth of the melody and the gravity of the lyrics combine to produce a rasa of awe and surrender.

'Jaya Jaya Bhagawati Lalite' is a sublime hymn to the Divine Mother, specifically in Her aspect as Lalita Tripura Sundari. This bhajan stands as a luminous ode to Shakti—the primordial feminine power. The literary structure is deeply anchored in the Shakta tradition, echoing the Lalita Sahasranama (1008 names of Mother Goddess) and invoking the goddess with names filled with meaning, like 'Bhagawati,' 'Lalite,' 'Sundari,' and

'Rajarajeshwari.' The language is both sensuous and spiritual, using poetic alliteration and rich epithets to draw the listener into the presence of the Mother. Sri Swamiji often sets this bhajan in Raga Kalyani, a raga that balances grandeur with grace. Kalyani is especially suited for Devi worship as it evokes both majesty and compassion. The ascending and descending notes carry an expansive and luminous quality, reinforcing the bhajan's invocation of the supreme beauty and sovereignty of the goddess. In performance, the slow build of melody and rhythm becomes a mirror of the rising kundalini—a subtle yet powerful awakening of Shakti within the listener.

Finally, 'Kanakaligaya Vedalingaya Vai Namaha' is a powerful and rare invocation to Lord Shiva in the form of Kanaka Linga—a golden, resplendent symbol of the Absolute. The very title blends the symbolic (kanaka = gold) and the transcendental (Veda = knowledge, Linga = formless reality with form). This bhajan is perhaps the most tantric in spirit among the five, rich with esoteric meaning. Sri Swamiji employs a unique blend of Sanskrit and classical Telugu/Kannada-rooted phrasing, creating a dense, resonant chant. The literary tone is reverent, authoritative, and mystical, placing the devotee before the luminous form of Shiva, who is both the object of worship and the inner Self. Musically, the bhajan often unfolds in Raga Bhairavi or Raga Revati, both of which are traditionally associated with intense devotion, spiritual longing, and ascetic beauty. These ragas help convey the majesty of the formless Shiva through a melody that is austere yet filled with longing. The slow, deliberate enunciation of the words, combined with the modal gravity of the raga, creates a deep meditative field for the listener, ideal for japa, puja, or inner contemplation.

These five bhajans—though varied in theme, style, and emotion—offer a comprehensive glimpse into Sri Swamiji's genius as a composer, poet, and spiritual guide. He tailors each melody and poetic line with surgical precision, ensuring that the bhava (feeling), raga (melody), and tattva (truth) are all perfectly aligned. Each composition is more than a song; it is a portal—a sacred vibration that carries the seeker inward toward the Divine. Whether calling out in childlike simplicity, soaring through Vedic heights, or diving deep into mystical symbolism, Sri Swamiji's bhajans continue to transform lives through the alchemy of sacred sound.

I end this section of the chapter with 'Nadenu Sandhīyatam'—a bhajan composed and performed by Sri Swamiji, featured in the album 'Keertana Chandrika.'[55] This composition exemplifies Sri Swamiji's profound integration of lyrical depth and musical sophistication, serving as a conduit for spiritual elevation. Lyrically, the bhajan is an earnest invocation, with the phrase 'Nadenu Sandhīyatam' translating to 'May the sound be united.' This reflects the essence of Nāda Yoga, emphasizing the union of the individual self with the universal through sacred sound. The lyrics are crafted to guide the listener toward inner harmony and a deeper connection with the Divine. Musically, Sri Swamiji employs a raga that complements the bhajan's contemplative nature. The melody is characterized by a serene tempo and fluid transitions, creating an atmosphere conducive to meditation. The rhythmic patterns are deliberately understated, allowing the melody and lyrics to take precedence, thereby facilitating a tranquil and immersive experience for the listener.

---

55. *Keertana Chandrika* is an 80-song album by Sri Ganapathy Sachchidananda Swamiji, released in 2022. One can listen to it on Apple Music and Spotify. Sri Swamiji has composed and performed Navavarana Kirtanas, which are devotional songs dedicated to the Divine Mother. These compositions have been performed during Navaratri celebrations and other spiritual events. For instance, during the Navavarana Puja, musical offerings are made by artists performing these compositions. Additionally, the Sarvepalli Sisters have performed 'Tripure Trigune,' a Navavarana composition by Sri Swamiji.

The composition's impact is profound as it encapsulates Sri Swamiji's philosophy of Nāda Chikitsa (healing through sound). Listeners often report a sense of inner peace and heightened spiritual awareness when engaging with this bhajan. The deliberate fusion of meaningful lyrics with a soothing melodic structure exemplifies Sri Swamiji's mastery in utilizing music as a tool for spiritual and emotional healing.

'Nadenu Sandhīyatam' stands as a testament to Sri Ganapathy Sachchidananda Swamiji's unique ability to blend lyrical profundity with musical elegance. The bhajan not only showcases his compositional prowess but also serves as a medium for imparting spiritual wisdom and promoting inner tranquility among listeners.

The above section is an appetizer before the main course. Let us now attempt to (shall I say dare to?) examine the philosophic depth, range, musical splendor, devotion and meditational value, symbolism, and key themes that Sri Swamiji has infused in His compositions or bhajans. Again, here, the dilemma is which bhajans to choose from the 3,000 or more compositions available. I choose the following eight bhajans encompassing the principal ministrations of divinity in Hinduism.

i. I start with '**Rama Harē Jaya Shaurē**' again. This composition in Mayamaḷavagauḷa ragam and Adi talam is a devotional hymn to Lord Rama. It reflects surrender, philosophical depth, and an aspiration for spiritual liberation.

Pallavi

Rama Harē Jaya Shaurē

O Rama, the compassionate one (Harē), and the valiant (Shaurē), victory to You!

Sthapaya Maṁ Tava Tīrē

Establish me on the shores of Your divine grace, freeing me from the ocean of samsara.

▲ *85-foot-tall Hanuman in Trinidad*

◄ *Karyasiddhi Hanuman in Avadhoota Datta Peetham, Mysuru*

▲ *Pujya Sri Ganapathy Sachchidananda Swamiji in Shuka Vana*

▲ *Pujya Sri Swamiji in Kishkindha Moolika Bonsai Garden*

◄ *Kishkindha Moolika Bonsai Garden, Avadhoota Datta Peetham*

▲ *Various facets of Pujya Sri Ganapathy Sachchidananda Swamiji*

▲ ***3 Honorary Doctorates:*** *. Vijayanagara Sri Krishnadevaraya University, Bellary, Karnataka, 2013; World Classical Tamil University, London, 2016; Dr. Gangubai Hanagal Music and Performing Arts University, Karnataka, 2023*

सत्यमेव जयते

प्रधान मंत्री

Prime Minister

New Delhi
श्रावण 20, शक संवत् 1944
11th August, 2022

Shri H.V. Prasad Ji,

I felt deeply touched to learn about 'Gita Sahasragala' event organised by Avadhoota Datta Peetham at Dallas, Texas on August 13, 2022.

Srimad Bhagavad Gita is a reservoir of timeless wisdom propounded by Bhagwan Shri Krishna for the welfare of humanity. His sublime message of performing one's duty and maintaining equanimity always provides us guidance.

For centuries, countless generations have drawn encouragement and nourishment from the deep insights provided by Srimad Bhagavad Gita. Future generations will continue to experience the immense benefits from this transformative set of instructions.

'Gita Sahasragala' carries forward the glorious Indian tradition of memorising and reciting our scriptures. The collective chanting before a global audience will create an environment of positivity around us that has been widely extolled in our culture.

May 'Gita Sahasragala' illuminate our minds and inspire mankind to tread the path shown by Srimad Bhagavad Gita. I am sure that Avadhoota Datta Peetham will continue to discharge its responsibilities towards the society under the benevolent guidance of Sri Ganapathy Sachchidananda Swamiji.

Best wishes to Avadhoota Datta Peetham for its endeavours.

(Narendra Modi)

Shri H.V. Prasad
Executive Trustee
Avadhoota Datta Peetham, USA

◀ *Honourable Prime Minister Sri Narendra Modi in Avadhoota Datta Peetham*

▲ *Nada Brahma Sri Ganapathy Sachchidananda Swamiji*

The Magnum Opus by Pujya Sri Swamiji on Raga Ragini Nadayoga ▶

Mouna Seminar: Silence and Nada, Switzerland, March 2025 ▶

◄ ▲ *Sahasragala Bhagawad Gita Parayana in USA, 2022*

Music for Meditation and Healing session in progress ►

▲ *A panoramic view of Nada Mandapa in Avadhoota Datta Peetham*

▲ *Music for Meditation and Healing in Royal Albert Hall, London, 2012*

▲ *Receiving blessings of Pujya Sri Swamiji in Avadhoota Datta Peetham*

▲ *Some of the Guinness World Records*

Anupallavi

Bhavadūrē Shrutisarē

Keep me far from the cycle of birth and death (bhava), O essence of the Vedas (shrutisara)!

Bhavaparē Gatavairē

Help me cross the ocean of existence and free me from enmity and ignorance.

Caraṇaṁ 1

Janmaahatai Ryadupattaṁ

The impurities (karma and attachments) accumulated over hundreds of lifetimes,

Kamasahasrai Ssampraptaṁ

And the desires born of thousands of cravings,

Vardhi Riva Praviahōṣyaṁ

May they be dried up like water evaporated from an ocean,

Tanmē Dhīmala Mapavahya

O Lord, cleanse these impurities (dhīmala) completely from my soul!

Caraṇaṁ 2

Tva Ccaraṇē Sthira Bhaktiṁ

Grant me unwavering devotion (sthira bhakti) to Your feet.

Tva Dvacanē Ghana Raktiṁ

Let my mind be deeply attached to Your words and teachings.

Tva Nmananē Mati Shaktiṁ

Empower me with strength of intellect to meditate upon You.

Kr̥paya Mayyabhi Sampadya

Through Your infinite grace, bless me with these virtues.

Caraṇaṁ 3

Janakasuta Samu Pētē

To You, who is united with Sīta, the daughter of King Janaka,

Hanuma Dupaahrita Padē
And whose feet are worshipped by Hanuman,
Saumitri Pratipūjyē
To You, revered even by Lakṣmaṇa (Saumitri),
Tvayi Madbuddhiṁ Sanyōjya
O Lord, direct my intellect to You alone!

Caraṇaṁ 4

Harimantrat Ra Varṇaṁ
From the Harī mantra comes the syllable 'Ra.'
Shivamantrat Ma Varṇaṁ
From the Shiva mantra comes the syllable 'Ma.'
Svīkurvan Samputitaṁ
Together, these form the Divine name Rama, which is all-encompassing.
Mahitaṁ Tvannamasjapya
O Lord, I chant Your revered name with devotion.

Caraṇaṁ 5

Vēdashirashcaya Saraṁ
You are the essence of the Upanishads, the crown jewel of the Vedas.
Bhēdakaḷa Pravidūraṁ
You are beyond duality and free from distinctions.
Saccidanandakaraṁ
You are the embodiment of existence, consciousness, and bliss (Saccidananda).
Tanmē Samyagbōdhayitva
O Lord, grant me the right knowledge and realization of this truth.

Essence and Key Themes

This hymn is a profound mix of devotion, self-reflection, and philosophy, with key themes as follows:

a. **Surrender:** The devotee repeatedly surrenders to Rama, asking to be freed from desires, ignorance, and samsara.

b. **Purification:** The composition emphasizes cleansing the soul of accumulated karmic impurities and attachments.

c. **Meditation on Rama's Name:** The blending of 'Ra' (Harī mantra) and 'ma' (Shiva mantra) reflects the universality of Rama's name.

d. **Realization:** The final goal is to achieve self-realization, experiencing Rama as Saccidananda.

e. **Union with the Divine:** The hymn portrays Rama not only as a personal deity but also as the ultimate truth beyond duality.

f. **Devotional Impact:** Similar to Tyagaraja's56 compositions, this hymn expresses both personal devotion and philosophical inquiry.

g. **Philosophical Depth:** Like Adi Shankaracharya's Bhaja Govindam or the Upanishadic verses, it emphasizes transcending duality and realizing bliss.

h. **Musicality:** Set in Mayamaḷavagauḷa, the hymn is meditative and emotionally evocative, enhancing its spiritual appeal.

ii. 'Shrīraja Rajēshi Kuru Satkr̥paṁ'

This hymn, part of the Navavaraṇa Kīrtanalu, is a meditative

56. Tyagaraja (1767–1847) was a legendary Carnatic music composer and saint, renowned for his devotional compositions dedicated to Lord Rama, primarily in Telugu. Considered one of the Trinity of Carnatic music alongside Muthuswami Dikshitar and Syama Sastri, his kritis blend lyrical beauty, deep spirituality, and intricate musicality, forming a cornerstone of South Indian classical music.

prayer to Shrī Lalita Tripurasundarī, the Supreme Goddess residing in the Shrīcakra. Set in Ṣaṇmukhapriya ragam and Adi talam, it invokes the goddess to bestow grace and guide the devotee toward ultimate realization.

Pallavi

Shrīraja Rajēshi - Kuru Satkr̥paṁ
O Queen of queens, bestow Your divine grace upon me!
Shrīcakravasasi - Hr̥di Mē Vasa
O Goddess who resides in the Shrīcakra, please take abode in my heart!

Anupallavi

Vishala Bha Vilasini - Nava Cakrantarvasini
O resplendent one, dwelling within the vast and luminous nine enclosures (Navacakra) of the Shrīcakra!
Sadaiva Tat Tat Surasvarūpē - Bhaktaḷī Dhī Dīpē
You embody the divine forms of the deities (Tat Tat Surasvarūpa) and serve as the guiding light for Your devoted followers.

Caraṇaṁ 1

Dēvīcakra Samaikyaṁ Mē - Cētasi Bhavayami
I meditate upon the unity of the Shrīcakra and its divine essence within my mind.
Cakrabrahmaṇḍai-kyaṁ Ca-cittē Nidadhami
I establish the oneness of the Shrīcakra with the cosmic universe (Brahmaṇḍa) in my consciousness.
Ajaṇḍapiṇḍaṁ-Ḍayō Rabhēdaṁ
I contemplate the unity of the macrocosm (Ajaṇḍa) and microcosm (Piṇḍa) without duality.
Bhavē Gaḍhaṁ Cintayē
I deeply reflect upon this profound truth.
Manōshca Dēvya Abhēda Rītiṁ

I hold firmly the inseparability of my mind and the Divine Mother
Praṇaspandair Dharayē
I sustain this awareness through the rhythm of my breath and life force.

Caraṇaṁ 2

Nadakara Tanō Shiva Vamasharīra Gatē
You are the embodiment of the primordial sound (nāda), residing in the left half of Shiva's body.
Vagarthakarē-bahu-vēdantē Pravicaryē
You are the unity of word (Vak) and meaning (Artha), extensively praised in the Vedanta.
Shivēsada-vidakr̥tē
You are Shiva's eternal consort, inseparable from Him.
Gajamukha Ṣaṇmukha Priyavahē
You are the mother of Gaṇapati (Gajamukha) and Ṣaṇmukha (Kartikeya), bestowing love upon them.
Tadartha Rūpē Tvamartha Dīpē
You manifest as the purpose (Tadartha) of existence and illuminate the ultimate meaning (Tvamartha).
Sacidanandē Bhayapahē
You are existence-consciousness-bliss (Saccidananda), dispelling all fear.

Key Themes and Symbolism:

a. **Shrīcakra57 and Navavaraṇa58**

57. The Śrīchakra, also known as the Śrīyantra, is a sacred geometric diagram composed of interlocking triangles, symbolizing the cosmos and the divine feminine energy of Devi Lalita Tripurasundari. It is used in Sri Vidya worship as a powerful tool for meditation, spiritual awakening, and invoking the unity of the macrocosm and microcosm.

58. Navāvaraṇa refers to the nine concentric enclosures or layers of the Śrīchakra, each representing a specific stage of spiritual evolution and an aspect of the Divine Mother. In Sri Vidya tradition, worship of the Navāvaraṇas involves

The hymn focuses on the Shrīcakra, representing the cosmic mandala of creation and the divine abode of Lalita.

The Navavaraṇa (nine enclosures) symbolizes the nine stages of spiritual realization, leading to liberation.

b. **Unity of Macrocosm and Microcosm**
The Ajaṇḍa (macrocosm) and Piṇḍa (microcosm) refer to the universality of the divine within all levels of existence.

The goddess bridges these realms, emphasizing the oneness of the individual and the cosmos.

c. **Divine Feminine and Shiva**
The goddess is described as Shiva's left half (Vamasharīra), highlighting their inseparability and the unity of masculine and feminine divine energies.

d. **Saccidananda**
Lalita is portrayed as the embodiment of existence (sat), consciousness (cit), and bliss (Ananda), symbolizing the ultimate goal of spiritual seekers.

e. **Meditative Depth**
The hymn reflects advanced meditative practices, such as uniting breath (praṇaspanda), thought, and cosmic awareness with the divine essence.

Depth of Philosophy: Similar to Muttuswami Dikshitar's Navavarṇa Kritis, this hymn integrates devotion with intricate esoteric and Vedantic concepts.

Musicality: The use of Ṣaṇmukhapriya ragam adds a contemplative and mystical tone, enhancing its spiritual appeal.

---

invoking various deities in each enclosure, culminating in the union with the ultimate reality, Śiva-Śakti at the central bindu.

Devotion and Meditation: The focus on merging individual consciousness with the divine is comparable to Adi Shankaracharya's Saundaryalahari.

'Shrīraja Rajēshi Kuru Satkṛpaṁ' is an extraordinary blend of devotion and meditative introspection. It guides the devotee from the external worship of the Shrīcakra to the internal realization of oneness with the Divine Mother, culminating in the ultimate state of blissful awareness. It is a masterpiece of spiritual and musical expression.

iii. 'Shivasati Vilasati'

This enchanting hymn, set in Sumanasarañjani ragam and Adi talam, celebrates the presence of Shiva and His divine consort Shakti in the devotee's heart. It is an expression of devotion, inner awakening, and spiritual bliss.

Pallavi

Shivasati Vilasati Mamahṛdi Tavabha
O Shiva, Your auspicious presence shines gloriously in my heart!
Pashupati Matimati Ramayati Kilaya
O Lord of all beings (Pashupati), Your intellect and grace bring joy and dissolve all bonds.

Caraṇaṁ 1

Vikasati Sarasija Mayimayi Sadayē
The lotus of divine grace blossoms in my heart, O compassionate one (Sadayē).
Sravatica Madhurasa Ihamamahṛdayē
The nectar of sweetness flows within my heart, filling it with bliss.
Sadayē Udayē Vijayē Abhayē
O compassionate one, bring forth enlightenment (Udaya), victory (Vijaya), and fearlessness (Abhaya).

Caraṇaṁ 2

Anupada Mudayati Nijasukha Mabhayē
Each step toward You reveals my innate joy and bestows fearlessness.
Avagati Vapuriha Mitihṛdi Kalayē
I realize Your form within me and meditate upon You in my heart.
Shamadē Damadē Vimadē Pramadē
You are the source of peace (Shama), control (Dama), humility (Vimada), and divine delight (Pramada).

Caraṇaṁ 3

Sumanisarañjani Raganilayē
You reside in the melody of Sumanasarañjani, the raga of beauty and grace.
Sacidanandai Rahamiha Vijayē
You embody existence, consciousness, and bliss (Saccidananda), and bring victory to my soul.
Vijayē Vimalē Vinutē Vanitē
O victorious one, O pure and radiant goddess, adored by all, consort of Shiva!

Key Themes and Symbolism

1. **Shiva's Presence in the Heart**
   The hymn repeatedly emphasizes Shiva's residence in the devotee's heart, symbolizing the union of the individual soul with the divine.

2. **Divine Grace and Bliss**
   The imagery of the blossoming lotus and flowing nectar reflects the transformative power of divine grace, bringing peace, joy, and enlightenment.

3. **Union of Shiva and Shakti**
   The reference to Vanitē (Shakti) highlights the inseparability of Shiva and Shakti, emphasizing their cosmic unity and balance.

4. **Philosophical Depth**
   The hymn explores key Vedantic concepts such as Saccidananda (existence-consciousness-bliss), aligning devotion with philosophical realization.

5. **Fearlessness and Victory**
   The invocation of fearlessness (Abhaya) and victory (Vijaya) represents the devotee's triumph over ignorance and obstacles through Shiva's grace.

6. **Musical Context**
   Sumanasarañjani Ragam: This ragam, known for its sweetness and uplifting tone, perfectly complements the hymn's themes of grace, joy, and devotion.

Adi Talam: The steady rhythm adds a meditative and contemplative flow to the composition, making it suitable for devotional singing.

Devotion and Philosophy: Like the Shiva Mahimna Stotram or Lingaṣṭakam, this hymn combines heartfelt devotion with deep philosophical insights.

Musical Appeal: The focus on the raga (Sumanasarañjani) adds a unique melodic dimension, distinguishing it from more traditional stotras.

'Shivasati Vilasati' is a beautiful and transformative hymn that invites the devotee to experience Shiva's grace and bliss within. Its combination of poetic beauty, spiritual philosophy, and musical charm makes it a timeless piece of devotion.

iv. 'Caṇḍī! Caṇḍasura Damani'
Ragam: Sindhubhairavi
Talam: Adi
Shlōkaṁ:
Yabhiṣṭuta Sapta Shatī-mantrēṇaṣṭambika Ca Ya|
Navadurgatmika Dadyat Thaṁ Mē Trithatigam||

Pallavi
Caṇḍī! Caṇḍasura Damani
Khaṇḍita Papa Bhava Janani
Caraṇaṁ:
Aṣṭa Matṛka Rūpiṇī!
Nava Durgakṛti Dhariṇī!
Durdama Bhaṇḍana Kariṇī!
Durmada Khaṇḍana Dhōraṇī! ...1
Saptashatī Manu Samstuta
Lalitakhyanē Prastuta
Dēvī Sūktai Rabhiṣṭuta
Tvaṁ Bhava Dēvī Mayi Mudita ...2
Aiṁ Hrīṁ Shrīṁ Manu Japatuṣṭa
Sarigama Padanī Svara Puṣṭa
Ōṅkaradbhuta Rava Ghuṣṭa
Saccidananda Sthiti Shiṣṭa ...3
Shlokaṁ:
"Yabhiṣṭuta Sapta Shatī-mantrēṇaṣṭambika Ca Ya|
Navadurgatmika Dadyat Thaṁ Mē Trithatigam||"

Meaning

May that Ambikā (Divine Mother), praised by the sacred 700 verses of the Devī Māhātmyam (Saptaśatī), and who manifests as the Navadurgā, grant me the threefold fruits (tritayatigam): dharma, artha, and kāma.

Philosophical Insight

This invokes the supreme Shakti praised in the Saptaśatī, affirming the belief in Divine Mother's ability to bestow the three human goals—righteousness, prosperity, and desires—implying that spiritual alignment brings material harmony.

Poetic Dimension

Classic Sanskrit meter, alliterative richness in "Sapta Shatī-mantrēṇaṣṭambika," invokes the rhythm of traditional stotra-style verses.

Musical Note

Reciting this over a soft alapana in Sindhubhairavi sets a deeply devotional and meditative tone, evoking reverence and surrender.

Pallavi

"Caṇḍī! Caṇḍasura Damani
Khaṇḍita Pāpa Bhava Janani"

Meaning

O Caṇḍī! Destroyer of the demon Caṇḍāsura, Mother who shatters sin and worldly bondage.

Philosophical Insight

This is a declaration of Devi as both fierce and compassionate—she destroys evil and liberates the soul from cycles of birth and sin (pāpa and bhava).

Poetic Note

Alliteration of "Caṇḍī! Caṇḍasura" and "Khaṇḍita...Janani" adds sonic force. The repetition reflects both reverence and immediacy.

Musical Treatment

The pallavi in Sindhubhairavi gains emotional intensity through its oscillations and gamakas, emphasizing Devi's majesty and compassion. Ideal for building bhakti-rasa.

Caraṇaṁ 1

"Aṣṭa Mātr̥ka Rūpiṇī!
Nava Durgakr̥ti Dhariṇī!
Durdama Bhaṇḍana Kariṇī!
Durmada Khaṇḍana Dhōraṇī!"

Meaning

You embody the eight divine mothers (Aṣṭa Mātr̥kās), take the form of the nine Durgās, destroy the unconquerable, and are the bearer of the mission to shatter pride and arrogance.

Reading

Here, Shakti is shown as multi-faceted—she is both maternal and martial. She is the force that subdues ego (durmada) and overcomes even the most formidable challenges (durdama).

Poetic Flourish

Note the parallel structure, repetition of "Dhariṇī / Kariṇī / Dhōraṇī"—this adds rhythmic cadence and mnemonic ease. The consonantal clusters evoke Devi's dynamism.

Musical Coloring

Sindhubhairavi's folk and semi-classical blend brings earthy power to these lines. The swaras can be played with expressive gamakas to mirror her fierce grace.

Caraṇaṁ 2

"Saptashatī Manu Samstuta

Lalitākhyānē Prastuta
Dēvī Sūktai Rabhiṣṭuta
Tvaṁ Bhava Dēvī Mayi Mudita"

Meaning

Praised in the Saptaśatī, spoken of in the Lalitā narrative, adored in the Devī Sūkta, may You, O Divine Mother, be joyfully present within me.

Philosophical Essence

This encapsulates the core of bhakti and Vedantic thought—the divine praised in sacred texts must also manifest within the devotee.

Poetic Strength

A literary salute to the three pillars of Shakta literature—Saptaśatī, Lalitā, Devī Sūkta. The verse moves from reverent listing to personal plea: Mayi Mudita.

Musical Flow

This section benefits from a slower lilt, allowing the bhava (emotion) to saturate each phrase. Ideal for bringing out Sindhubhairavi's emotive subtlety.

Caraṇaṁ 3

"Aiṁ Hrīṁ Shrīṁ Manu Japatuṣṭa
Sarigama Padanī Svara Puṣṭa
Ōṅkārād-bhuta Rava Ghuṣṭa
Saccidānanda Sthiti Shiṣṭa"

Meaning

Pleased by the chanting of the seed mantras Aiṁ Hrīṁ Shrīṁ, enriched by the swaras (sargam), resonant with the wondrous sound of Om, You abide as the pure existence-consciousness-bliss (sat-cit-ānanda) in the worthy.

Philosophical Depth

This is a masterful confluence of mantra, nāda (sound), and brahmajñāna. The Divine is both heard and felt; She is present in sound, syllable, and stillness.

Poetic Grace

Each line escalates spiritually: from mantra, to musical swaras, to Om, and finally to satcitānanda. It's a lyrical ladder to liberation.

Musical Highlight

A swara-based line like Sarigama Padanī Svara Puṣṭa invites creative sangatis (variations). A treat for performers and listeners alike to showcase laya-bhakti fusion.

"Caṇḍī! Caṇḍasura Damani" is an exalted hymn blending scriptural references, poetic beauty, and musical brilliance. The choice of Sindhubhairavi, with its rich emotional register and semi-classical flexibility, adds weight to the Devi's fierce and compassionate portrayals. The taal setting in Adi provides a familiar rhythmic base, allowing the lyrical structure to shine without complex rhythmic constraints.

Thematically, it journeys from invocation, praise, and theological exposition to deep personal longing and realization—thus making it not just a song, but a spiritual sādhana.

Caraṇaṁ 1

"Aṣṭa Mātṛka Rūpiṇī!
Nava Durgakṛti Dhariṇī!
Durdama Bhaṇḍana Kariṇī!

Durmada Khaṇḍana Dhōraṇī!"

Meaning

You embody the eight divine mothers (*Aṣṭa Mātr̥kās*), take the form of the nine Durgās, destroy the unconquerable, and are the bearer of the mission to shatter pride and arrogance.

Philosophical Reading

Here, Shakti is shown as multi-faceted—she is both maternal and martial. She is the force that subdues ego (*durmada*) and overcomes even the most formidable challenges (*durdama*).

Poetic Flourish

Note the parallel structure, repetition of "Dhariṇī / Kariṇī / Dhōraṇī"—this adds rhythmic cadence and mnemonic ease. The consonantal clusters evoke Devi's dynamism.

Musical Coloring

Sindhubhairavi's folk and semi-classical blend brings earthy power to these lines. The swaras can be played with expressive gamakas to mirror her fierce grace.

Caraṇaṁ 2

"Saptashatī Manu Samstuta
Lalitākhyānē Prastuta
Dēvī Sūktai Rabhiṣṭuta
Tvaṁ Bhava Dēvī Mayi Mudita"

Meaning

Praised in the Saptaśatī, spoken of in the Lalitā narrative, adored in the Devī Sūkta, may You, O Divine Mother, be joyfully present within me.

Philosophical Essence

This encapsulates the core of bhakti and Vedantic thought—the divine praised in sacred texts must also manifest *within* the devotee.

Poetic Strength

A literary salute to the three pillars of Shakta literature—*Saptaśatī*, *Lalitā*, *Devī Sūkta*. The verse moves from reverent listing to personal plea: *Mayi Mudita*.

Musical Flow

This section benefits from a slower lilt, allowing the bhava (emotion) to saturate each phrase. Ideal for bringing out Sindhubhairavi's emotive subtlety.

Caraṇaṁ 3

"Aiṁ Hrīṁ Shrīṁ Manu Japatuṣṭa
Sarigama Padanī Svara Puṣṭa
Ōṅkārād-bhuta Rava Ghuṣṭa
Saccidānanda Sthiti Shiṣṭa"

Meaning

Pleased by the chanting of the seed mantras *Aiṁ Hrīṁ Shrīṁ*, enriched by the swaras (*sargam*), resonant with the wondrous sound of Om, You abide as the pure existence-consciousness-bliss (*sat-cit-ānanda*) in the worthy.

Philosophical Depth

This is a masterful confluence of *mantra*, *nāda* (sound), and *brahmajñāna*. The Divine is both heard and felt; She is present in sound, syllable, and stillness.

Poetic Grace

Each line escalates spiritually: from mantra, to musical swaras, to

Om, and finally to *satcitānanda*. It's a lyrical ladder to liberation.

Musical Highlight

A swara-based line like *Sarigama Padanī Svara Puṣṭa* invites creative sangatis (variations). A treat for performers and listeners alike to showcase laya-bhakti fusion.

Conclusion

"Caṇḍī! Caṇḍasura Damani" is an exalted hymn blending scriptural references, poetic beauty, and musical brilliance. The choice of **Sindhubhairavi**, with its rich emotional register and semi-classical flexibility, adds weight to the Devi's fierce and compassionate portrayals. The taal setting in **Adi** provides a familiar rhythmic base, allowing the lyrical structure to shine without complex rhythmic constraints.

Thematically, it journeys from invocation, praise, and theological exposition to deep personal longing and realization—thus making it not just a song, but a spiritual *sādhana*.

Would you like a performance-style notated version or an audio-alapana suggestion as well?

v. Sentence-by-Sentence Meaning of the Composition: 'Dishi Dishi Saṁ Vasasi Vibhō'

Pallavi

Dishi Dishi Saṁ Vasasi Vibhō

O Lord! You reside in all directions (dishi dishi), pervading the entire universe!

Vasa Vasa Mē Hr̥di Shiva Bhō

O Shiva! Please come and dwell in my heart.

Girigiri Garjasi Puripuri Nr̥tyasi

You roar like thunder on the mountains and dance joyfully in the cities.

Girishara Hē! Purahara Bhō
O Girisha (Lord of the Mountain Kailssa), O Purahara (Destroyer of the demon Tripura), I bow to You!

Caraṇaṁ 1

Andhatvaṁ Hē Andhaka Hsrin - Hara Hara Mē
O Hara! You destroy ignorance (andhatvaṁ) just as you destroyed the demon Andhaka. Please dispel my darkness (ignorance).
Dr̥shamacchsṁ Drak Dishamē Svamin - Shubhagati Vitaraṇa
O Master (Svamin), quickly grant me divine vision (dr̥shaṁ) and show me the auspicious path (shubhagati).
Mata Tatō Dēvī Dēvō - Pravilasataṁ
May the divine Mother and Father, Shakti and Shiva, shine gloriously within me.
Mama Dr̥k Cakrē Mama Dhīmargē - Pravimala Guṇayuji
Illuminate my inner vision (dr̥k cakra) and intellect (dhīmarga) with pure and virtuous qualities.

Caraṇaṁ 2

Tīvrad Yōgat Dhvastahantaṁ - Kuru Kuru Maṁ
Through the power of intense yoga, destroy (dhvasta) my ego and the sense of "I" (ahantaṁ). Transform me completely!
Vishadē Jñanē Tvatha Mē Cittaṁ - Ratamapi Kurukuru
O Lord, guide my mind (cittaṁ) to remain immersed (ratam) in pure and clear knowledge (vishada jñana).
Shūlagrē Tē Lagnaṁ Bhavat - Kurukuru Maṁ
Anchor me (maṁ) firmly at the tip of Your trident (shūlagra) with unwavering devotion.
Triguṇatītaṁ Samayatītaṁ - Viracaya Viracaya
Take me beyond the three guṇas (sattva, rajas, tamas) and the bounds of time (samaya). Grant me transcendence!

Caraṇaṁ 3

Kalatīta Tvaṁ Vai Marō - Harasi Jagat

You are beyond time (kala) and destroy the delusion of the world (jagat). O Shiva, You are eternal!

Tanusaundaryē Nanu Marastvaṁ - Sumadhura Rucidhara

In the beauty of Your divine form (tanusaundarya), You embody Kama (desire) and sweetness (sumadhura).

Maranmarō Jayandōḷa - Rasi Hi Dvidha

O Destroyer of Kama (Mara), Your joyous movements (Jayandōḷa) create a dual experience of ecstasy and realization.

Satataṁ Sa Tvaṁ SacidAnandō - Hṛdi Mama Jayajaya

You are the eternal existence-consciousness-bliss (Saccidananda). Reside in my heart forever—Victory to You!

This composition is a poetic and philosophical prayer to Lord Shiva. It celebrates His cosmic presence, divine beauty, and the destruction of ignorance and ego. The devotee seeks Shiva's guidance to transcend material limitations and to dwell in blissful union with the eternal Saccidananda. Each line resonates with deep devotion and philosophical insight, inviting Shiva into the heart while striving for liberation and enlightenment.

vi. 'Jaya Jaya Bhagavati Lalitē, Janani Sadashiva Militē'

Victory to you, O Goddess Lalita, the Supreme Mother!

You are the consort of Lord Sadashiva, always united with him in divine harmony.

Meaning: The Pallavi celebrates the goddess's supreme divinity and her inseparable union with Lord Shiva, symbolizing the union of energy (Shakti) and consciousness (Shiva).

Caraṇaṁ 1

Janma Jaramṛti Rahitē

Bhagavati Tavaka Caraṇaṁ
Bhavatu SadAmama Sharaṇaṁ
You are beyond birth, aging, and death, eternal and infinite.
O Divine Mother, may your lotus feet always be my eternal refuge.
Meaning: This verse praises the goddess as transcendent and beyond the limitations of worldly existence, emphasizing her role as the ultimate savior for her devotees.

Caraṇaṁ 2
Bhaṇḍartitasura Nūtē, Kuṇḍalisa Muditē
Caṇḍa Karayuta Kantē
You are worshipped by gods like Indra, whom you protected when Bhandasura attacked.
Your brilliance is equal to the light of a thousand suns.
Indu Kalañcita Maulē, Nandana Samakr̥ta Malē
You wear the crescent moon on your crown.
Garlands offered by the celestial beings (Gandharvas) adorn you.
Sindhūraṅkita Phalē, Sundara Mukura Kaphēlē
Your forehead is adorned with sindoor (vermilion).
Your face is a perfect reflection of beauty, like a mirror.
Meaning: This verse highlights her celestial beauty and her role as the protector of the heavens and her devotees.

Caraṇaṁ 3
Taṭaṅkita Mihirē, Taṭamaṇi Kuṇḍala Raēcirē
Your earrings shine like the sun.
Your ear ornaments are studded with radiant gems.
Taraka Nasikahīrē, Tamradharamaṇi Sarē
Your nose stud sparkles like a star.
Your lips are red and radiant, like copper.
Kundala Sadr̥sha Sunalē, Kambusadr̥ggali Nalē

Your cheeks are smooth and rounded like a lotus bud.
Your neck is graceful like a conch shell.
Kōmala Bahu Mṛṇalē, Kaṇṭhala Sanmaṇi Malē
Your arms are soft and tender, like a lotus stalk.
Your neck is adorned with a garland of precious gems.
Meaning: This verse is a vivid description of the goddess's divine form, emphasizing her ornaments and physical grace, which captivate her devotees.

Caraṇaṁ 4

Nīyōtpaladala Nayanē, Nīrajari Punamavadanē
Your eyes resemble blue lotus petals.
Your face shines like the full moon amidst a lotus pond.
Nayana Sujīvita Madanē, Nirmala Manasa Sadanē
Your enchanting eyes revive the spirit of Kamadeva (the god of love).
You reside in the pure and serene hearts of your devotees.
Pashaṅkushadharacapē, Rashadhika Pararūpē
You wield the noose, goad, and bow in your hands.
You are the most exalted and radiant form of divine energy.
Rashajayapaṭu Rūpē, Ashamitana Tapapē
Your form surpasses all in splendor.
You relieve the sufferings of those longing for you.
Meaning: This verse highlights her beauty, her weapons symbolizing control over the material world, and her power to dispel suffering.

Caraṇaṁ 5

Hari Payōdhara Kōsha, Harishayanōdara Dēshē
Your bosom holds treasures of divine nectar.
Your navel resembles the abode of Lord Vishnu (Hari).
Harihayagōpanikashē, Hṛdavalīvinivēshē
You shine in the radiance of Vishnu's divine light.

You reside in the innermost hearts of your devotees.
Rasarasa Sīnibhanabhē, Rashanakr̥ta Shivalōbhē
Your navel is beautiful and enchanting, like a serene pool.
Your waist is adorned with ornaments that captivate even Shiva.
Ruciràmbara Kaṭishōbhē, Ratigr̥havibhajagha Nabhē
Your attire enhances the beauty of your waist.
You are the goddess of love and beauty, dwelling in the heart of Shiva.
Meaning: This verse portrays her as the ultimate symbol of beauty and love, residing in the divine presence of Lord Shiva and Vishnu.

Caraṇaṁ 6

Karaṭikarōru Sujanaa, Kaṅkṣita Varasuradhēnō
Your thighs are perfect and strong, inspiring devotees.
You are like the wish-fulfilling cow (Kamadhenu) for those who seek you.
Kamalapadaruṇabhanō, Kulimaladavakr̥shanō
Your feet radiate a red glow like the rising sun.
You burn away the impurities of the world like wildfire.
Mayē Muraharanide, Madhuvada Viracida Bhadrē
O Mother of Maya, you defeated Madhu and Kaitabha.
You are the protector who grants auspiciousness to your devotees.
Marita Kaiṭabha Vīrē, Mahiṣaniṣūdana Dhīrē
You slayed the demons Kaitabha and Mahishasura.
You are the embodiment of courage and strength.
Meaning: This verse focuses on her role as the protector of the universe, emphasizing her strength and ability to destroy evil forces.

Caraṇaṁ 7

Dhūshaṇḍē, Darita Caṇḍaka Muṇḍē

You destroyed Dhumralochana and crushed Chanda and Munda.
Nashita Rudhirajaṣaṇḍē, Bhūṣita Shashidhara Khaṇḍē
You annihilated the armies of Raktabija.
You adorn the crescent moon on your crown.
Sūdita Shumbhanishumbhē, Mōdita Vibudhakadambē
You defeated Shumbha and Nishumbha.
You delight the celestial beings with your victories.
Khaditaripunikurumbē, Bhrajitaravishatabimbē
You crushed the hordes of your enemies.
You shine brilliantly like the radiance of a hundred suns.
Meaning: This verse glorifies her victorious battles against the most fearsome demons, establishing her as the ultimate protector of dharma.

Caraṇaṁ 8

Bhavabhaya Varidhi Taraṇaṁ, Bhavukavitaraṇa Nipuṇaṁ
You help your devotees cross the ocean of worldly fears.
You inspire the greatest poets with your divine presence.
Bhavavidhi Pūjita Caraṇaṁ, Bhavadapimataphala Sharaṇaṁ
Your feet are worshipped by Brahma and other gods.
You grant liberation to those who seek refuge in you.
Sakala Caracara Mūrtē, Sarasijabhavanutakīrtē
You are the essence of all moving and non-moving things in creation.
Your glory is praised by Brahma, the lotus-born creator.
Sadhita Natabhavajūrtē, Sadhitanaravara Pūrtē
You fulfill the desires of devotees and relieve their sorrows.
You bless the best among men with spiritual and material fulfillment.
Meaning: The final charanam portrays her as the compassionate mother, granting liberation, inspiration, and fulfillment to all her devotees.

vii. 'Shambhō! Samba! Stutiriha Tē,' is a beautiful tribute, featuring a profound blend of devotion, lyrical elegance, and melodic richness. Set in the ragam Hēmavati and talam Adi, the piece invokes the glory of Lord Shiva (Shambhō, Samba), celebrating his benevolent and powerful aspects. Here's a brief interpretation of each section:

Pallavi

The Pallavi reverberates with an earnest call to Shambhō and Samba, praising their supreme nature. The devotee, acknowledging their grace and the reverence of divine beings, speaks of Shiva's playful yet world-protecting nature that brings auspiciousness to the devotees.

Interpretation

- **Shambhō! Samba! Stutiriha Tē:** 'Oh Shambhō, Samba! This hymn is in your praise.'

- **Nata Sugatē! Suranuta! Tē:** 'You, who are worshipped by the noble and extolled by the celestials.'

- **Hasatē Lasatē Jagadapaharatē:** 'Who playfully shines and alleviates the world's sorrows.'

- **Jayatē Bhavatē Shubhamanu Diahatē:** 'You triumph and bestow blessings upon your devotees.'

Anupallavi

The Anupallavi deepens the adoration by emphasizing Lord Shiva's protective, gracious, and radiant qualities. It also reflects on his powerful attributes that embody both fierce and nurturing aspects.

Interpretation

- **Sajjana Sharaṇa! Samhṛta Karaṇa!:** 'Refuge of the virtuous!

You bring an end to destruction!'

- **Rucira Caraṇa! Shubha Caraṇa!:** 'Your feet are resplendent and bring auspiciousness.'

- **Bhujagabharaṇa! Suvikaraṇa!:** 'Adorned with serpents, you possess magnificent arms.'

Caraṇaṁ

The Caraṇam paints an intimate and reflective portrayal of devotion. The devotee seeks the Lord's divine presence in their heart and describes the daily rituals and the simplicity of their sincere worship.

Interpretation of Stanzas

1. **First Stanza**
    - **Mamaka Hr̥dayē Vikasatu Tē:** 'May your sacred beauty blossom in my heart.'
    - **Pavana Shōbha Sujana Gatē!:** 'You, whose pure splendor is the path of the righteous.'
    - **Santata Karuṇa! Samhr̥ta Maraṇa!:** 'Ever compassionate, conqueror of death.'
    - **Vimata Varaṇa! Vipula Raṇa!:** 'Conqueror of the disbelievers, hero of great battles.'
    - **Vimala Sphuraṇa! Viṣadharaṇa!:** 'Pure brilliance, bearer of venom.'

2. **Second Stanza**
    - **Tavaka Sutanū Rmama Puratō:** 'May your divine form appear before me.'
    - **Dainika Pūja Japa Vidhitō:** 'Through my daily rituals and chants.'

- **Dīvyatu Vimala Dīpyatu Sukala:** 'May the pure, divine energy glow radiantly.'
- **Mr̥duhaimavatī Yuti Tarala:** 'Flowing gently in union with Parvati, the daughter of Himavan.'
- **Sacidananda Kr̥ti Sarala:** 'Embodiment of truth and bliss, your creation is straightforward.'

This composition exemplifies a heartfelt devotional expression, perfect for evoking deep reflection and worship during renditions in the Hēmavati ragam, known for its serene and uplifting quality.

viii. This composition titled '**Nikhila Nilaya Mantraṁ'** is set in the raga Shrīrañjani and follows the Adi tala. The composition reveres the sacred mantra of Lord Rama, highlighting its transformative and liberating power. Each verse emphasizes how the Rama Mantra is a force of protection, liberation, and the ultimate truth.

Meaning and Explanation of the Verses:

Verse 1

Nikhila Nilaya Mantraṁ - Nitya Tattvakhya Mantraṁ

'The mantra that resides in everything, the eternal mantra representing the highest truth.'

Bhavakulahara Mantraṁ - Bhūmija Praṇa Mantraṁ

'The mantra that destroys the sorrow of worldly existence, the life force of Sita (Bhūmija).'

Pavanajanuta Mantraṁ - Parvatī Mōkṣa Mantraṁ

'The mantra praised by Hanuman (son of the wind), the mantra that grants liberation to Parvati.'

Pashupati Nija Mantraṁ - Patumaṁ Rama Mantraṁ

'The mantra dear to Lord Shiva (Pashupati), may the Rama mantra protect me.'

Verse 2

Praṇavanilaya Mantraṁ - Praṇa Nirvaṇa Mantraṁ

'The mantra residing in the primal sound "Om," the mantra that leads to the liberation of the soul.'

Prakr̥tipuruṣa Mantraṁ - Brahmarudrēndra Mantraṁ

'The mantra representing both nature and the supreme spirit, the mantra adored by Brahma, Rudra, and Indra.'

Prakaṭa Durita Raga - Dvēṣa Nirṇasha Mantraṁ

'The mantra that dispels overt suffering, attachments, and hatred.'

Raghupati Nija Mantraṁ - Ramaramēti Mantrah

'The mantra of Lord Rama himself, the powerful "Rama, Rama" mantra.'

Verse 3

Jayatu Jayatu Mantraṁ - Janmasaphalya Mantraṁ

'Victory to the mantra, the mantra that makes life successful.'

Janana Maraṇa Khēda - Klēsha Vicchēda Mantraṁ

'The mantra that ends the cycle of birth and death, removing all suffering and distress.'

Sakala Nigama Mantraṁ - Sarvashastraika Mantraṁ

'The mantra found in all scriptures, the one mantra that encompasses all sacred teachings.'

Raghupati Nija Mantraṁ - Ramaramēti Mantraṁ

'The mantra of Lord Rama, the sacred "Rama, Rama" mantra.'

This shlōka expresses deep devotion to the Rama mantra, underlining its potency in achieving spiritual liberation, dispelling worldly sufferings, and bringing ultimate peace. It reveres the mantra as a source of universal truth and the key to transcending the material world.

The bhajan compositions of Sri Ganapathy Sachchidananda Swamiji are not merely devotional songs—they are sacred architectures of sound designed to purify the heart, awaken the intellect, and uplift the soul. Each bhajan carries a unique vibration that reflects Sri Swamiji's deep yogic vision and spontaneous spiritual insight, combining the rigor of classical music with the subtlety of divine inspiration. Each of His compositions effortlessly blends the name of the Raga chosen by Him into the lyrics. From invoking the compassionate presence of Rama and the majestic energy of Lalita to dissolving the ego before Lord Shiva and contemplating the power of sacred mantras, these compositions guide the seeker through the full spectrum of spiritual experience—devotion (bhakti), knowledge (jnana), introspection (dhyana), and transcendence (moksha). The musical choices—from the selection of raga and tala to the pacing and melodic contour—are never arbitrary; they are chosen to resonate with the spiritual intent of the lyrics, ensuring that the listener is gently ushered into a higher state of consciousness. In this light, Sri Swamiji's compositions emerge as timeless tools of transformation, offering both the intimacy of personal prayer and the grandeur of cosmic celebration. They are aural sanctuaries where sound becomes sacred, and music becomes the language of liberation.

References

1. www.sgs-ragasagara.com-raga-ragini-nāda-yoga
2. www.dattapeetham.org-bhajans and healing music : bhajanamala.
3. YouTube: September 21, 2019; May 20, 2014; July 16, 2019; June 21, 2010; September 30, 2018; June 6, 2010; March 3, 2011.
4. Apple Music-web player.
5. www.music.apple.com
6. www.open.spotify.com-nāda himalaya
7. www.rachaelathomasj.com
8. www.sgsashrams.org
9. www.facebook.com – 5 February 2024.

CHAPTER 11

Living Sanctuaries: The Eco-spiritual Vision of Sri Ganapathy Sachchidananda Swamiji Through Kishkindha Moolika Bonsai Garden and Shuka Vana

Abstract

This chapter explores two extraordinary eco-spiritual projects conceived and nurtured by His Holiness Sri Ganapathy Sachchidananda Swamiji at Avadhoota Datta Peetham, Mysuru—Kishkindha[59] *Moolika Bonsai Garden and Shuka Vana. Far more than environmental initiatives, these sacred spaces embody a synthesis of spiritual philosophy, ecological awareness, compassionate action, and aesthetic refinement. Kishkindha is a miniature forest where the ancient art of bonsai becomes a metaphor for yogic discipline and inner transformation. Shuka Vana is a sanctuary for over two thousand rescued parrots, a healing refuge for both birds*

59. The Kishkindha garden in the Ramayana holds great significance as the serene and sacred setting where Lord Rama forms his alliance with Hanuman and Sugriva, marking the beginning of the Vanara army's quest to find Sita. It symbolizes the turning point from sorrow to action, as Rama's divine mission gains momentum amidst the lush, spiritually charged landscape of Kishkindha.

and human visitors, and a living expression of the Vedic principle of reverence for all beings. Through these living sanctuaries, Sri Swamiji demonstrates how ecology and spirituality are not separate pursuits but intertwined expressions of divine love and dharmic responsibility. This chapter presents a comprehensive narrative of their background, concept, symbolic resonance, ecological value, and national and international recognition.

~

The Kishkindha Moolika Bonsai Garden, nestled within the serene and spiritually vibrant precincts of Avadhoota Datta Peetham in Mysuru, is one of the most unique and inspiring manifestations of Sri Ganapathy Sachchidananda Swamiji's vision to integrate nature, spirituality, and education into a unified experience. More than a horticultural exhibit, the Kishkindha Bonsai Garden represents a living testimony to Sri Swamiji's profound reverence for all life forms and His enduring commitment to environmental consciousness, ecological stewardship, and spiritual symbolism.

The very name 'Kishkindha' evokes sacred associations. In the Ramayana, Kishkindha is the monkey kingdom ruled by Sugriva and Hanuman, a place of divine encounters, deep forests, and spiritual transformation. Sri Swamiji deliberately chose this name for the bonsai garden to indicate the playful, sacred, and powerful nature of the space. Just as the forest of Kishkindha served as a setting for devotion, loyalty, and awakening, the garden also serves as a spiritual forest in miniature, where each tree is not merely a plant but a silent rishi radiating life, patience, and stillness.

The concept of the bonsai garden aligns seamlessly with Sri Swamiji's broader teachings on inner growth, self-discipline, and the cultivation of stillness through restraint. In the art of bonsai, the tree is lovingly trained over many years to grow within limits, adapting itself into a beautiful, balanced form that harmonizes with its container. This mirrors the yogic path, wherein the human being, through self-control and inner refinement, transforms the vast energy of life into something inwardly majestic. Each bonsai, therefore, becomes a metaphor for spiritual sadhana—growth through discipline, beauty through humility, and grandeur through silence.

The Kishkindha Bonsai Garden is one of the largest of its kind in India and one of the few bonsai collections in the world curated under a spiritual leader. The garden is home to over 450 carefully nurtured bonsai specimens, representing both indigenous and exotic species. Some of the trees are decades old, meticulously shaped by Sri Swamiji's guidance and by trained disciples and horticulturalists who consider their work to be a form of worship. Each tree is labeled with its botanical name, common name, and spiritual or mythological significance, enabling visitors to experience the space not only as a visual delight but as a walk through the sacred teachings of nature.

The garden's layout follows a narrative path, with themed sections representing aspects of Indian mythology, planetary energies, and elemental principles. Trees representing deities like Ganesha, Shiva, Vishnu, and Hanuman are placed with intentional symmetry and symbolism. For example, a strong, upward-reaching ficus may be placed as a representation of Lord Hanuman's unwavering strength and humility. A gnarled, weathered tree may embody the resilience of sages. The result is a sacred grove in miniature—a forest that speaks not through noise but through silence and presence.

The significance of Kishkindha Bonsai Garden lies not only in its aesthetic and symbolic appeal but also in its educational and ecological value. Thousands of schoolchildren, students, environmentalists, and spiritual seekers visit the garden annually. For the younger generation, it serves as an introduction to the delicate balance of ecology and the art of preservation. For seekers and devotees, it is a meditative space—a living 'mandala' where the mind naturally slows down, attention deepens, and a reverence for life takes root. Sri Swamiji has often emphasized that spending time with trees can restore mental balance and emotional clarity, and the garden offers precisely such a therapeutic environment.

Over the years, the garden has received national and international recognition. It has been listed among India's top thematic gardens and has received accolades from horticultural societies and environmental organizations. Sri Swamiji Himself has been lauded as an ambassador of nature preservation and botanical education, and the Kishkindha Garden remains one of the key attractions during the Ashrama's annual celebrations and festivals. The garden has also inspired other spiritual and botanical institutions to initiate similar projects that blend natural art forms with sacred pedagogy.

In essence, the Kishkindha Moolika Bonsai Garden is far more than a curated collection of miniature trees. It is a living scripture, where each leaf, branch, and root tells a story—not only of nature's resilience and artistry but of the human soul's potential for transformation. In the hands of Sri Ganapathy Sachchidananda Swamiji, the bonsai becomes a sacred form—not stunted, but refined; not limited, but elevated. The garden stands as a spiritual ecosystem where nāda (sound), yoga (discipline), and prakriti (nature) converge, inviting every visitor into a gentle but profound encounter with the sacred. Now, let me come to the other dimension and vision of Sri Swamiji—the Shuka Vana.

Among the many remarkable manifestations of Sri Ganapathy Sachchidananda Swamiji's compassionate and visionary leadership, Shuka Vana, located within the sacred grounds of Avadhoota Datta Peetham in Mysuru, stands as a pioneering center for avian care, ecological awareness, and spiritual education. It is not merely a sanctuary for parrots—it is a sanctuary for the conscience of humanity, a living symbol of the deep Vedic teaching that the Divine resides equally in all beings, including those who cannot speak for themselves in human language. Established by Sri Swamiji out of boundless love for the speechless and the winged, Shuka Vana is a unique fusion of science, seva, spirituality, and sanctity.

The very name 'Shuka Vana'—meaning 'the Forest of Parrots'—has deep symbolic and scriptural resonance. In the Puranic and Vedantic traditions, the parrot (shuka) is not just a bird but a revered figure. Shuka Maharishi, the son of Sage Vyasa and the narrator of the *Bhagavata Purana*,[60] is often depicted in iconography and lore as a divine parrot, symbolizing pure knowledge, uninterrupted japa, and the bridge between moksha and bhakti. By invoking this ancient association, Sri Swamiji infused the sanctuary not only with ecological purpose but with spiritual gravity, positioning Shuka Vana as a place of both rescue and revelation.

The background of Shuka Vana's establishment lies in Sri Swamiji's long-standing relationship with birds, particularly parrots. Recognizing their high sensitivity, cognitive abilities, and emotional intelligence, Sri Swamiji began sheltering and healing rescued and abandoned birds many years ago. What began as a quiet act of compassion gradually grew into a full-fledged avian rehabilitation center, built with sophisticated infrastructure and medical facilities to care for

---

60. *Bhagavata Purana* or *Srimad Bhagavatam* is one of Hinduism's 18 major puranas, comprising nearly 18,000 verses across twelve books or cantos. It focuses on the life and teachings of Krishna Bhagawan, presenting a comprehensive narrative that includes cosmology, theology, mythology, and legends and is highly regarded for its emphasis on devotion or bhakti to Bhagawan Krishna as the supreme being.

injured, orphaned, and mistreated birds, especially exotic and endangered species. Today, Shuka Vana houses over 2,100 rare, endangered, and exotic parrots and other species, making it one of the largest and most diverse bird aviaries in the world, both in terms of numbers and species variety.

The concept behind Shuka Vana is multilayered. It is, first and foremost, a rehabilitation and rescue center staffed by trained veterinarians, ornithologists, and caretakers who provide specialized medical treatment, nutrition, and a safe, enriched environment for the birds to heal and thrive. But beyond that, it is a spiritual ecology project, where each bird species is associated with a particular deity, planetary influence (Navagraha), or nakshatra (birth star). Sri Swamiji has painstakingly compiled a parrot astrology matrix, wherein each species is mapped to a specific cosmic force, allowing devotees and visitors to connect with birds that correspond to their own spiritual or astrological inclinations. This visionary system is not superstition—it is a revival of the Vedic understanding of the interconnectedness of life, karma, and cosmic harmony.

Sri Swamiji's profound connection with nature and wildlife, rooted in his upbringing in the jungles of Mekedatu, inspired the creation of Shuka Vana. His early experiences amidst rich biodiversity instilled in him a deep respect for all living beings, motivating his ongoing efforts to promote harmony between humans and nature. At Shuka Vana, the well-being of its avian residents is of paramount importance. The birds are housed in a meticulously designed, two-layered meshed aviary that provides a natural and protective environment, complete with selected plants and trees. Their diet is carefully curated to ensure balanced nutrition, including fresh fruits like apples, papayas, and kiwis; vegetables such as carrots and pumpkins; sprouts; nuts; seeds; and specialized hand-feeding formulas. Food preparation takes place in the 'Phala Shala,' where processes like cleaning, cutting, and sprouting are conducted under stringent quality controls.

The aviary is supported by a dedicated team of approximately 70 caretakers, including resident veterinarians, biochemistry and genetic technologists, trained avian medical caregivers, and volunteers. Routine health check-ups are conducted every 45 days to monitor the birds' well-being. Those diagnosed with illnesses are isolated in 'Sanjeevini Vana,' the quarantine facility, and receive tailored treatments based on sensitivity tests. The attached avian hospital is equipped with advanced diagnostic tools, including radiology units, ultrasound machines, and biochemistry analyzers, ensuring comprehensive medical care. Beyond rehabilitation, Shuka Vana plays a crucial role in the conservation of endangered and critically endangered species, such as the blue-throated macaw and the lesser sulfur-crested cockatoo. By providing a safe habitat conducive to breeding, the center contributes significantly to the preservation of these species. Additionally, Shuka Vana serves as an educational hub, raising public awareness about avian conservation through interactive experiences. Visitors have the unique opportunity to observe rare parrot species up close and even interact with them, fostering a deeper appreciation for these magnificent creatures. Through Shuka Vana, Sri Ganapathy Sachchidananda Swamiji exemplifies the profound impact of compassionate action, creating a harmonious sanctuary where humans and birds coexist in mutual respect and care.

Visitors to Shuka Vana do not experience a zoo-like setting but a sacred interaction with nature. The aviaries are meticulously maintained, with trees, flowers, and water bodies designed to replicate natural habitats. The birds are not confined but protected, and their vibrant presence fills the atmosphere with color, sound, and life. This environment itself becomes a meditative space where one witnesses the dignity of life in all its forms and reflects on the responsibility humans carry as caretakers of the earth. A dedicated team of doctors and facilities for basic pathological tests, treatment, and rehabilitation contribute to the care of the parrots, especially the injured or those that may have taken ill.

The significance of Shuka Vana extends into several spheres—ecological, educational, medical, and spiritual. Ecologically, it contributes to the preservation of biodiversity, especially for parrot species under threat from habitat loss and illegal trafficking. Educationally, it functions as a center for environmental awareness, where children and adults alike are introduced to the ethics of conservation, the intelligence of birds, and the importance of compassion. It also inspires future scientists and naturalists by showing how spiritual leadership can drive innovation in animal welfare.

Shuka Vana has received widespread national and international recognition for its pioneering work. Most notably, it was awarded the Guinness World Record for the most bird species in an aviary, a formal acknowledgment of the scope and scale of the initiative. It has been featured in environmental conferences, spiritual forums, and animal welfare discussions, attracting the attention of ecologists, wildlife experts, and policymakers. Yet, beyond accolades, its true recognition lies in the thousands of lives it has saved—feathered lives often forgotten by society yet held sacred by Sri Swamiji.

Sri Swamiji's guiding principle in establishing Shuka Vana is rooted in the Vedantic maxim: 'Sarva bhuta hite ratah'—those who delight in the welfare of all beings. He has often said that listening to birds, caring for them, and simply being in their presence has a calming, healing effect on the human nervous system. In this light, Shuka Vana is not just a rescue center for birds—it is also a healing center for humans, reminding us of our shared destiny with all living creatures and inviting us to rediscover reverence, responsibility, and the joy of silent service.

Shuka Vana represents a remarkable confluence of ancient wisdom and modern compassion, a space where ecological restoration becomes an act of spiritual practice. Through this sanctuary, Sri Ganapathy Sachchidananda Swamiji has shown the world that divinity is not locked in temples alone but lives in forests, nests, and feathers. Shuka Vana is thus a voice for the voiceless, a forest for the forgotten, and, ultimately, a living shrine to divine love in its most unconditional form.

In an era increasingly marked by ecological degradation and spiritual disconnect, the Kishkindha Moolika Bonsai Garden and Shuka Vana stand as luminous examples of what is possible when ancient wisdom meets compassionate action. These sanctuaries, envisioned and nurtured by Sri Ganapathy Sachchidananda Swamiji, transcend the boundaries of religion, science, and art to reveal a deeper truth—that all life is sacred and that nature is not separate from the divine but one of its purest expressions. Through bonsai trees that teach patience and stillness and parrots that remind us of the beauty of speech and song, Sri Swamiji has created not monuments but living scriptures, inviting each visitor to read, reflect, and revere.

In these spaces, we are not merely spectators—we are participants in a sacred ecology, a dharma that embraces all life forms in compassion and joy. Whether standing beneath a miniature peepal (banyan) tree in Kishkindha or listening to the vibrant calls of birds in Shuka Vana, one encounters the same message: to live in harmony is to live in grace, and to care for creation is to care for the Creator within us all.

References

1. www.borrbo.com, 25 September 2023.
2. www.dattapeetham.org
3. www.tripadvisor.com, 2025.
4. www.youtube.com, 23 October 2014.
5. www.trivago.com – sgs birds-shuka vana.
6. www.travelerstories.com
7. www.travelwithbrij.wordpress.com

CHAPTER 12

The Significance of Avadhoota Lineage of Bhagawan Dattatreya and Sri Ganapathy Sachchidananda Swamiji

Abstract

The Avadhoota lineage is among the most esoteric and spiritually exalted lineages in the Indian yogic and philosophical tradition, rooted in the timeless wisdom of Bhagawan Dattatreya—the primordial Guru and the archetype of ultimate renunciation and divine omniscience. This chapter explores the historical, metaphysical, and experiential contours of the Avadhoota path within the Dattatreya sampradaya, elucidating its emphasis on spontaneous knowledge (sahaja jnana), inner detachment, and cosmic integration. Against this sacred backdrop, the life and mission of Sri Ganapathy Sachchidananda Swamiji are situated as a radiant and accessible embodiment of the ancient Avadhoota ideal in the modern age. Through His silence and song, His healing music, and global spiritual work, Sri Swamiji carries forward the flame of Bhagawan Dattatreya's wisdom while reinterpreting it for contemporary seekers. This chapter thus presents an integrated vision of the Avadhoota lineage, culminating in the unique contribution of Sri Swamiji as both a torchbearer and transformer of this luminous tradition.

The Avadhoota lineage represents one of the most profound currents in the spiritual history of India—a stream of awakened beings who have transcended worldly dualities and social constructs to abide in the pure awareness of the Self. This lineage finds its fountainhead in Bhagawan Dattatreya, a deity revered not as a mythological figure alone but as a living symbol of unity among the triadic powers of Brahma, Vishnu, and Shiva. Bhagawan Dattatreya, as described in scriptures such as the *Avadhoota Gita* and the *Tripura Rahasya*, embodies the spontaneous state of one who has realized the Self without conflict, effort, or dependence on outer form. He is the original Avadhoota—one who lives beyond the mandates of orthodoxy, flowing in perfect harmony with the inner dictates of cosmic intelligence.

In classical texts like the *Srimad Bhagavatam* (11.7), Bhagawan Dattatreya appears before King Yadu and expounds the teachings of the twenty-four gurus—symbolic representations of natural phenomena, animals, and human experiences that, for the realized sage, become mirrors of the Absolute. This view of the world as an open scripture is central to the Avadhoota perspective, where wisdom is drawn not from doctrine but from direct experiential insight. An Avadhoota is thus not defined by external appearance but by inner disidentification from body, mind, and ego and an unwavering establishment in the Self.

The Dattatreya tradition flourished over millennia through various lineages—among them the Nath Sampradaya, with figures like Gorakhnath and Jnaneshwar and the Kaula Tantric schools. However, the Avadhoota tradition remains unique in its insistence on inner sovereignty over outer ritual, inward freedom over social recognition, and the spontaneous transmission of knowledge over formal instruction. It is within this sacred continuum that Sri Ganapathy Sachchidananda Swamiji must be understood.

Sri Swamiji stands not merely as a spiritual teacher but as a realized being in the Avadhoota tradition—*one who operates from a state of inner detachment while engaging dynamically with the world.* Born in 1942 in the lineage of revered yoginis and siddhas, Sri Swamiji, through his life, reveals the classic marks of an Avadhoota: an early awakening, complete detachment from worldly ambition, profound silence punctuated by spontaneous teaching, and a mission that transcends sectarian boundaries. Like Bhagawan Dattatreya, who roamed the forests and deserts with no fixed abode, Sri Swamiji travels the world spreading healing, wisdom, and love—yet remains unattached to any personal identity or institutional construct.

What makes Sri Swamiji's manifestation especially significant is how He embodies the Avadhoota path in a form accessible to the modern seeker. Unlike the classical Avadhoota, who remained aloof from society, Sri Swamiji embraces technology, organizes healing concerts, builds temples and ashrams, and even appears before scientific audiences—all while remaining centered in the stillness of the Self. His compositions, bhajans, and meditative ragas are not artistic expressions alone but vibrational transmissions of Nāda Brahma, echoing the silence of the sages through the music of the Divine. In this, He is reminiscent of Bhagawan Dattatreya's own teachings, where sound, nature, and inner intuition become the pathways to realization.

Moreover, the iconography and teachings at the Avadhoota Datta Peetham in Mysuru, established by Sri Swamiji, are deeply infused with Bhagawan Dattatreya's essence. The presence of the universal Guru Dattatreya in His triple form, the Hanuman temple symbolizing inner strength, and the sacred sculptures and chants—all point toward a living lineage that does not replicate the past but regenerates it in new form. The Datta Kriya Yoga and Nāda Chikitsa programs designed by Sri Swamiji function as direct channels for spiritual and psychological transformation, much like the spontaneous guidance offered by Bhagawan Dattatreya to seekers like King Yadu or Parashurama.

Importantly, Sri Swamiji's state as an Avadhoota is not merely conferred by tradition but confirmed by direct experience. Thousands of devotees attest to His ability to read minds, cure illnesses, and dissolve karmic patterns through silent blessings or melodic utterances. This mystery, this inscrutable grace, is the hallmark of the Avadhoota—a being who has no agenda, no ego, and no worldly ambition yet radiates the light of the infinite. The author of the *Avadhoota Gita* proclaims: 'I am neither the doer nor the enjoyer…I am pure consciousness alone.' Sri Swamiji, through His life and teachings, demonstrates this in wordless clarity.

In contextualizing His significance, we can thus see Sri Ganapathy Sachchidananda Swamiji not merely as a saint or guru but as a re-manifestation of the Dattatreya consciousness—a living Avadhoota who bridges the ancient with the contemporary, the silent with the sung, and the formless with the compassionate form. He is the needed presence of the Avadhoota principle in an age that hungers for spiritual authenticity without rigidity, mystical experience without dogma, and divine love without condition.

The Avadhoota lineage of Bhagawan Dattatreya represents a sacred thread of experiential wisdom, stretching from the primordial forests of ancient India to the globalized ashrams and digital realms of the 21st century. In this luminous lineage, Sri Ganapathy Sachchidananda Swamiji shines as a contemporary embodiment of the Avadhoota ideal—*living not outside the world but untouched by it, offering the world not escape but inner transformation*. His music, silence, healing, and teachings are not separate disciplines but integrated expressions of the same unshakable awareness rooted in Bhagawan Dattatreya's truth.

As the Avadhoota is one who is beyond labels and boundaries, Sri Swamiji's life becomes a lesson in transcendence itself. In Him, we do not merely witness a teacher—we encounter the teaching, the path, and the goal. He is both the river and the shore, the sound and the silence, the Avadhoota and the Atman. Through Him, the timeless current of Bhagawan Dattatreya flows on—unbroken, unbounded, and eternally free.

References

1. Avadhoota Datta Peetham. (n.d.). *Sri Ganapathy Sachchidananda Swamiji – Life and Mission.* Mysuru, India: Avadhoota Datta Peetham Publications. Retrieved from https://www.dattapeetham.org

2. Avadhoota Datta Peetham. (n.d.). *Avadhoota Datta Peetham: Ashrama and Global Mission.* Retrieved from https://www.dattapeetham.org/page/view/about-ashrama

3. Avadhoota Datta Peetham. (n.d.). *Nāda Chikitsa – Music for Meditation and Healing.* Retrieved from https://www.dattapeetham.org/page/view/bhajans-and-healing-music

4. Avadhoota Datta Peetham. (n.d.). *Datta Kriya Yoga: Yogic Breathing for Physical and Spiritual Well-being.* Retrieved from https://www.dattapeetham.org/page/view/datta-kriya-yoga

5. Sri Ganapathy Sachchidananda Swamiji. (n.d.). *Discourses on Bhagavata, Datta Darshana, and Avadhoota Gita.* Mysuru, India: Datta Publications.

6. Sri Ganapathy Sachchidananda Swamiji. (2005). *Guru Gita: With Commentary by Sri Swamiji.* Mysuru: Datta Peetham Publications.

7. Sri Ganapathy Sachchidananda Swamiji. (n.d.). *Teachings on the Twenty-Four Gurus of Dattatreya.* Audio and Video Discourses. Retrieved from https://www.youtube.com/@SGSMMS

8. *Srimad Bhagavatam* (*Bhagavata Purana*), Canto 11, Chapter 7. (Trans. Swami Tapasyananda, 1980). Chennai, India: Ramakrishna Math.

9. *Tripura Rahasya*. (Trans. Swami Sri Ramanananda Saraswathi, 2001). Tiruvannamalai, India: Sri Ramanasramam.
10.*Avadhoota Gita*. (Trans. Swami Ashokananda, 1982). Kolkata: Advaita Ashrama.
11.Sundar, A. (2012). *Avadhoota Datta Peetham: A Modern Spiritual Institution*. In Contemporary Hindu Spirituality (pp. 157–175). Delhi: Bharatiya Vidya Bhavan.
12.White, D.G. (1996). *The Alchemical Body: Siddha Traditions in Medieval India*. Chicago: University of Chicago Press. [For contextual history on the Avadhoota and Nath traditions]
13.Joshi, L. (1982). *Studies in the Origins of Indian Mysticism*. Delhi: Motilal Banarsidass.

CHAPTER 13

The Global Impact of Sri Ganapathy Sachchidananda Swamiji's Mass Recitations: A Journey Towards World Peace

Abstract

Sri Ganapathy Sachchidananda Swamiji has profoundly influenced global spiritual consciousness through orchestrating mass recitations of sacred Hindu texts, notably the Bhagavad Gita[61] *and the Hanuman Chalisa.*[62] *His initiatives have not only fostered communal harmony and*

---

61. The *Bhagavad Gita* is a 700-verse sacred Hindu scripture that forms part of the Indian epic *Mahabhharata.* Presented as a dialogue between Lord Krishna and the warrior prince Arjuna on the battlefield of Kurukshetra, the Gita addresses profound philosophical and ethical dilemmas. As Arjuna hesitates to fight in a war against his own kin, Krishna imparts timeless teachings on duty (dharma), selfless action (karma yoga), devotion (bhakti yoga), and spiritual wisdom (jnana yoga). The *Bhagavad Gita* transcends religious boundaries and offers guidance for righteous living, inner peace, and self-realization.

62. The Hanuman Chalisa is a revered 40-verse devotional hymn dedicated to Lord Hanuman, composed by the 16th-century saint and poet Tulsidas in Awadhi. Rich in poetic beauty and spiritual depth, the Chalisa praises Hanuman's

spiritual awakening but have also achieved international recognition, setting multiple Guinness World Records. This chapter delves into the background, purpose, and achievements of Sri Swamiji's endeavors, highlighting their significance in promoting universal peace and cultural unity.

In an era marked by rapid globalization and cultural amalgamation, the preservation and promotion of spiritual traditions serve as vital conduits for fostering global harmony. Sri Ganapathy Sachchidananda Swamiji has emerged as a beacon of spiritual enlightenment, dedicating His life to the propagation of ancient wisdom through music, meditation, and mass recitations. His initiatives aim to harness the collective energy of communal chanting to instill peace, unity, and spiritual awareness across diverse populations.

Mass recitations have long been integral to Hindu spiritual practice, serving as mediums for communal participation and the amplification of spiritual vibrations. Texts like the *Bhagavad Gita* and the Hanuman Chalisa hold profound significance within Hinduism—the former encapsulating philosophical dialogues on duty and righteousness and the latter venerating Hanuman, symbolizing strength and devotion. Sri Swamiji's vision to organize large-scale recitations of these texts stems from a desire to rejuvenate these traditions, making them accessible and relevant in the contemporary world.

---

strength, wisdom, devotion, and heroic deeds, especially his unwavering service to Lord Rama. Reciting the Hanuman Chalisa is believed to bestow courage, remove obstacles, and protect devotees from harm and negativity. Its rhythmic verses and profound meanings have made it one of the most widely chanted and cherished hymns in Hinduism, inspiring faith, devotion, and inner strength across generations.

The primary objectives behind Sri Swamiji's mass recitations encompass spiritual upliftment through engaging individuals in collective chanting to elevate personal and communal spiritual consciousness besides helping promote world peace by utilizing the harmonious vibrations generated through mass recitations to promote global tranquility and reduce societal discord. These initiatives also serve to safeguard and revitalize ancient scriptures and practices by integrating them into modern community activities, fostering a sense of unity and shared purpose among participants from diverse backgrounds.

Sri Swamiji's exhortations have garnered international acclaim, culminating in several Guinness World Records that underscore the global impact of his work:

i. **Largest Simultaneous Hindu Text Recital:** On August 13, 2022, under Sri Swamiji's guidance, approximately 2,000 devotees from 13 countries gathered at the Allen Event Center in Texas, USA, to recite the entire 700 verses of the *Srimad Bhagavad Gita*. This event was recognized by Guinness World Records as the largest simultaneous Hindu text recital.

ii. **Most People Chanting at a Single Venue:** On January 31, 2015, in Tenali, Andhra Pradesh, India, Sri Swamiji led 1,28,918 participants in chanting the Hanuman Chalisa, setting a world record for the largest gathering for chanting at a single location.

iii. **Longest Continuous Chanting of Hanuman Chalisa:** In December 2024, over 650 devotees, guided by Sri Swamiji, engaged in a marathon Hanuman Chalisa chanting session lasting 33 hours, 33 minutes, and 33 seconds at Nāda Mandapa in the Avadhoota Datta Peetham, Mysuru. This feat established a new Guinness World Record for continuous chanting.

iv. **Largest Online Video Album of People Chanting:** By July 31, 2016, Sri Swamiji achieved a Guinness World Record for compiling 40,976 videos of individuals chanting the Hanuman Chalisa, reflecting the extensive reach of his spiritual mission.

The mass recitations organized by Sri Swamiji have had multifaceted impacts:

- **Spiritual Resonance:** Participants often report profound personal transformations, attributing enhanced inner peace and clarity to the collective chanting experience.
- **Global Unity:** By bringing together individuals from various cultural and national backgrounds, these events exemplify the unifying power of shared spiritual practices.
- **Cultural Revival:** The recitations serve as a bridge connecting younger generations to ancient traditions, ensuring the continuity and relevance of sacred texts in modern times.
- **Recognition and Inspiration:** The acknowledgment by Guinness World Records not only honors Sri Swamiji's efforts but also inspires other spiritual leaders and communities to undertake similar initiatives.

Sri Ganapathy Sachchidananda Swamiji's orchestration of mass *Bhagavad Gita* and Hanuman Chalisa recitations thus represents a harmonious blend of devotion, cultural preservation, and global outreach. Through these monumental gatherings, He has demonstrated the profound impact of collective spiritual practice in fostering peace and unity worldwide. The international recognition of these efforts underscores the timeless relevance of ancient wisdom and the enduring power of communal harmony in addressing contemporary challenges.

References

1. Avadhoota Datta Peetham. (n.d.). *Mass Chanting Events and World Records.* Mysuru, India: Datta Peetham Archives. Retrieved from https://www.dattapeetham.org

2. Avadhoota Datta Peetham. (n.d.). *Sri Swamiji's Global Gita Parayana and Hanuman Chalisa Chanting Events.* Retrieved from https://www.dattapeetham.org/page/view/special-events

3. Avadhoota Datta Peetham. (2022, August 13). *Guinness World Record for Largest Hindu Text Recital* (*Bhagavad Gita*). Allen, Texas: Press Release.

4. Avadhoota Datta Peetham. (2015, January 31). *Hanuman Chalisa Chanting in Tenali – Guinness World Record with 1,28,918 Participants.* Mysuru: Datta Peetham News Desk.

5. Avadhoota Datta Peetham. (2024, December). 33:33:33 *Hanuman Chalisa Marathon at Nāda Mantapa, Mysuru.* Mysuru: Official Program Archive. [Unpublished internal release]

6. Guinness World Records. (n.d.). *Most People Chanting at a Single Venue – Hanuman Chalisa, Tenali, India.* Retrieved from https://www.guinnessworldrecords.com

7. Guinness World Records. (n.d.). *Largest Online Video Album of People Chanting – Hanuman Chalisa, 2016.* Retrieved from https://www.guinnessworldrecords.com

8. News India Times. (2023, December 5). *Sri Ganapathy Sachchidananda Swamiji Performs Healing Ragas at Carnegie Hall.* Retrieved from https://www.newsindiatimes.com

9. Sundar, A (2012). *Avadhoota Datta Peetham and Global Hindu Spiritual Movements.* In Contemporary Hindu Spirituality (pp. 162–174). Delhi: Bharatiya Vidya Bhavan.

CHAPTER 14

Empowering the Differently-abled: Initiatives of Pujya Sri Ganapathy Sachchidananda Swamiji

Abstract

Pujya Sri Ganapathy Sachchidananda Swamiji has dedicated His life to the holistic upliftment of humanity. Among His numerous humanitarian endeavors, His commitment to assisting differently-abled individuals stands out prominently. Through financial assistance, provision of essential implements, and support for specialized institutions like the SGS Vagdevi Integrated School in Bengaluru, Sri Swamiji has significantly enhanced the lives of many. This chapter delves into these initiatives, highlighting their impact and the profound compassion that drives them.

In a world where differently-abled individuals often face societal and infrastructural challenges, the compassionate interventions of spiritual leaders can bring about transformative change. Pujya Sri Ganapathy Sachchidananda Swamiji exemplifies this ethos, intertwining spiritual guidance with tangible support for those in need. His initiatives for the differently-abled are not mere acts of charity but are rooted in a deep-seated belief in the inherent divinity and potential within every individual.

Recognizing the mobility challenges faced by many differently-abled individuals, Sri Swamiji has consistently provided financial aid and essential implements to enhance their quality of life. A notable instance of this commitment was during His 82nd birthday celebrations in May 2024. On this occasion, Sri Swamiji distributed 82 pieces of equipment, including 40 wheelchairs, eight walkers, ten crutches, and five sticks, to specially-abled persons. This act not only addressed their immediate physical needs but also symbolized His unwavering dedication to their well-being.

Such distributions are a regular feature of Sri Swamiji's philanthropic activities. Every year, during His birthday celebrations, calipers, wheelchairs, sewing machines for self-employment, and other tools are provided to those in need. This consistent support underscores His belief in empowering individuals to lead independent and dignified lives.

Education serves as a cornerstone for empowerment, especially for differently-abled children. Sri Swamiji's vision materialized in the form of the SGS Vagdevi Integrated School in Girinagar, Bengaluru. Maintained and managed by the SGS Ashram, this institution offers comprehensive services, including diagnosis, evaluation, early intervention, and educational programs tailored for communication-impaired children. The school's integrated setup ensures that these children receive holistic support, encompassing academic instruction, vocational training, and social integration skills.

The mission of the SGS Vagdevi Centre is to empower hearing and communication-impaired individuals through developmental initiatives such as identification, diagnosis, early intervention, and educational intervention. By focusing on these areas, the institution aims to bridge the communication gap and facilitate the seamless integration of these individuals into mainstream society.

Sri Swamiji's compassion extends beyond the differently-abled. He has established various social welfare projects under the aegis of Avadhoota Datta Peetham. One such initiative is Amma Vodi (Mother' lap), a destitute women's rehabilitation center in Hyderabad, which provides shelter and care for elderly women aged 70 and above. Additionally, the ashram supports over 1,800 students by improving educational infrastructure and providing necessary resources. These endeavors reflect Sri Swamiji's holistic approach to societal upliftment, addressing both physical and spiritual needs.

Pujya Sri Ganapathy Sachchidananda Swamiji's initiatives for the differently-abled exemplify a harmonious blend of spiritual wisdom and compassionate action. By providing financial assistance, essential implements, and supporting specialized educational institutions, He has illuminated the path towards an inclusive society where every individual, regardless of physical limitations, can realize their full potential. His unwavering commitment serves as an enduring inspiration, reminding us of the profound impact that empathy and dedicated service can have on the lives of others.

References

1. Avadhoota Datta Peetham. (n.d.). *Humanitarian Services: Support for Differently-Abled and Destitute Women.* Mysuru, India: Official Publications. Retrieved from https://www.dattapeetham.org/page/view/social-welfare-activities
2. Avadhoota Datta Peetham. (2024, May). *82nd Birthday Celebrations*

of Sri Ganapathy Sachchidananda Swamiji: Distribution of Aids to Specially-Abled Individuals. Mysuru: Datta Peetham Media Reports.

3. Avadhoota Datta Peetham. (n.d.). *SGS Vagdevi Centre for the Communication Impaired. Bengaluru: Official Project Page.* Retrieved from https://www.sgsashram.org/vagdevi

4. SGS Vagdevi Integrated School. (n.d.). *Institutional Profile and Services. Bengaluru: Internal Reports and Educational Program Overview.*

5. Datta Peetham News Desk. (2022). *Sri Swamiji's Social Initiatives: Annual Report on Aid Distribution, Educational Support, and Women's Rehabilitation Projects.* Mysuru: DYC Publications.

6. Avadhoota Datta Peetham. (n.d.). *Amma Vodi: Rehabilitation Center for Destitute Women. Hyderabad: Datta Peetham Welfare Division.* Retrieved from https://www.dattapeetham.org/page/view/amma-vodi

7. Sundar, A. (2012). *Contemporary Hindu Spirituality: Case Study of Avadhoota Datta Peetham's Social and Spiritual Impact.* In Contemporary Hindu Spirituality (pp. 169–174). Delhi: Bharatiya Vidya Bhavan.

8. Times of India. (2024, May 26). *Sri Ganapathy Sachchidananda Swamiji Celebrates 82nd Birthday with Aid to Differently-Abled.* Bengaluru Edition.

9. The Hindu. (2018, June 22). *SGS Vagdevi Centre Helps Communication-Impaired Children Integrate into Mainstream Schools.* Retrieved from https://www.thehindu.com

CHAPTER 15

Sri Ganapathy Sachchidananda Swamiji's Global Temples: Living Symbols of Service, Unity, and Healing

Abstract

This chapter is the story of how one spiritual master—Sri Ganapathy Sachchidananda Swamiji—used temples not just as places of worship but as engines of social good, healing, and harmony. Whether it is the towering 85-foot Hanuman idol in Trinidad, the buzzing Karya Siddhi Hanuman Temple in Dallas, or the serene Nāda Mandapa[63] *and unique temples within the Mysuru Ashram, each project carries a larger purpose. These are not just architectural wonders or devotional hotspots—they bring people together, offer comfort during life's storms, and encourage values like service, unity, and cultural pride. Sri Swamiji's temples act as beacons of hope across the world, reminding people that spirituality*

63. Nāda Mandapa is a sanctified music hall or spiritual sound pavilion within the ashram complex, where divine music (nāda) is performed as an offering to the Divine. The term combines Nāda—the primordial sound or sacred vibration that underlies all creation, central to Indian spiritual and musical traditions and Maṇḍapa—a pillared hall or pavilion used for spiritual gatherings, rituals, or ceremonies.

is not about isolation—it is about uplifting others, healing hearts, and building strong, compassionate communities.

Let me start with the 85-foot Hanuman idol in Trinidad, which represents strength that unites people. In 1999, something remarkable happened in Trinidad and Tobago. A towering 85-foot Hanuman idol—the tallest in the Western Hemisphere—was unveiled under the guidance of Sri Ganapathy Sachchidananda Swamiji. But this wasn't just a spiritual milestone—it was a moment of cultural revival and social awakening. For generations, the Indian diaspora in Trinidad had held fast to their traditions but struggled for a space that truly reflected their collective strength. Sri Swamiji's vision gave them more than a monument. It gave them identity, pride, and unity.

Located at the Dattatreya Yoga Centre in Carapichaima, the idol became a rallying point for the entire Hindu community across the Caribbean. The idol stands not just as an icon of devotion but as a symbol of resilience, reminding people of the values of service, discipline, and inner strength that Hanuman represents. Over time, the site has evolved into a center for social cohesion, interfaith respect, and community welfare—bridging generations and backgrounds through shared reverence and public service.

Now, let me come to the Karya Siddhi[64] Hanuman Temple in Frisco, Dallas, which is nothing but faith in action and community in motion. In the heart of Texas, in the fast-growing city of Frisco near Dallas, stands a temple that pulses with energy

64. Karya Siddhi (Sanskrit: कार्यसिद्धि) translates to 'successful completion of a task' or 'fulfillment of a goal/desire' in English.

Karya = work, task, goal, or undertaking; Siddhi = accomplishment, success, or attainment.

and purpose—the Karya Siddhi Hanuman Temple. Established by Sri Swamiji, this temple is much more than a spiritual retreat for Indian Americans. It is a hub of community life, a place where culture, compassion, and public service go hand in hand.

Here, children learn Sanskrit and classical arts, young professionals find grounding through spiritual values, and families come together in celebration and service. From food drives and health camps to youth leadership and music therapy programs, the temple has become a model for how spirituality can serve the real-world needs of modern society. The temple welcomes all with open arms—creating harmony among cultures while staying rooted in the timeless teachings of Sanatana Dharma.

The faith here is alive, dynamic, and result-oriented. People come with hopes, take vows (sankalpas), and return with gratitude. Sri Swamiji's vision was clear: build a temple where people don't just pray but also grow, give back, and connect deeply with others.

How can one not mention the Nāda Mandapa, Mysuru, which is a symbol of healing through sound and harmony through culture? Nestled in the Mysuru Ashram is a hall (not a closed auditorium) that doesn't just echo music—it radiates healing. The Nāda Mandapa, created by Sri Swamiji, is a unique space where sound becomes medicine. Through carefully designed concerts and ragas, Sri Swamiji has brought ancient Indian music back into the limelight—not as entertainment but as a form of therapy for the body and soul. In this hall, music is a community affair. The Global Hanuman Chalisa Parayana held here brought thousands together in collective chanting, generating waves of positive energy. The Mandapa also hosts musical performances that cross cultural and linguistic barriers, uniting people through the universal language of sound.

The real magic of Nāda Mandapa lies in how it turns culture into care. It is where the science of vibration meets the soul of tradition, helping people deal with stress, pain, and isolation in today's fast-paced world. It is Sri Swamiji's answer to a global need for peace—through the timeless power of nāda (sound). It is a structure unlike any other—a place where architecture, acoustics, tradition, and transcendence come together. The Nāda Mandapa is not merely a concert hall. It is a sanctified space where music transforms into prayer, where sound vibrations become tools of healing, and where art is elevated to its highest purpose—uplifting the human spirit.

One of the defining features of the Nāda Mandapa is its impeccable acoustics. The hall has been engineered to carry the subtle nuances of classical music without the need for artificial amplification, allowing natural sound to fill the space with remarkable clarity and resonance. Sri Swamiji was personally involved in guiding the hall's design, ensuring that it would enhance the purity of musical notes and allow audiences to immerse themselves fully in the sonic experience. The result is an 'auditorium' that is equally suitable for the delicate 'gamakas' [65] of a Carnatic 'alapana[66],' the dynamic improvisations of Hindustani 'khayal[67],' the grandeur of

---

65. Gamakas in Carnatic music are the oscillations, slides, and embellishments applied to notes that give each raga its distinct identity and emotional depth. They are essential expressive techniques that transform plain notes into rich, nuanced musical phrases.

66. Alapana in Carnatic music is an improvised, rhythm-free exploration of a raga, showcasing its essence and emotional mood without lyrics or tala (beat). It allows the musician to creatively unfold the raga's melodic beauty, often serving as a prelude to a composed piece.

67. Khayal in Hindustani music is a prominent vocal genre known for its improvisational freedom and emotional expression, built around a short lyrical

Western orchestration, and even Swamiji's own meditative healing ragas.

What further sets the Nāda Mandapa apart is its interior gallery—a remarkable tribute to the masters of world music. Along its walls are beautifully framed portraits of musical legends from every tradition and era. From the great doyens of Carnatic music like Saint Tyagaraja, Muthuswami Dikshitar and Shyama Shastri to Hindustani music icons, their images gaze down with a quiet dignity. Sri Swamiji has also ensured that the hall honors Western classical giants like Beethoven, Mozart, and Tchaikovsky, reminding every visitor that music knows no boundaries—linguistic, cultural, or religious. These portraits serve not merely as decoration but as silent witnesses to a tradition of seva through music. They bless every performance that unfolds beneath their gaze and inspire younger generations to aspire to that same level of dedication and excellence.

Since its inauguration in 1999, the Nāda Mandapa has hosted an extraordinary array of acclaimed musicians and musicologists from India and around the world. It has become a prestigious stage where maestros render their art not for applause but as an offering of devotion and service (seva). Among those who have graced its stage are Pundit Bhimsen Joshi, Pundit Jasraj, Dr Mangalampalli Balamuralikrishna, the legendary violinist Dr L. Subramaniam, the flute virtuoso Pt Hariprasad Chaurasia, mridangam maestro Umayalapuram K. Sivaraman, tabla genius Ustad Zakir Hussain, and several doyens of vocal music including Bombay Jayashri, Aruna Sairam, and Sudha Ragunathan. Hindustani greats like Pt Vishwa Mohan Bhatt, Pt Ulhas Kashalkar, Kaushiki Chakraborty, and Mahesh Kale have also offered their music here. Notably, the hall has

---

composition. It allows the artist to explore a raga deeply through slow (vilambit) and fast (drut) tempos, using intricate ornamentations like taans, gamakas, and meends.

welcomed collaborative ensembles that blend Indian classical with jazz, world music, and Western symphonic styles, all under the patronage and encouragement of Sri Swamiji, whose own musical vision embraces the full spectrum of sonic expression.

Sri Swamiji Himself is central to the spiritual energy of the Nāda Mandapa. As a pioneering exponent of Music for Meditation and Healing, He has performed over a hundred therapeutic concerts in this very hall, drawing audiences from across the globe. His concerts, deeply intuitive and guided by inner inspiration, utilize specific ragas to balance the body's energies and uplift the mind. The healing vibrations generated during these events are often described by devotees as deeply transformative, capable of reducing stress, relieving pain, and awakening inner peace.

The Nāda Mandapa is more than a performance venue—it is a temple of sound, where the divine is invoked not through ritual alone but through the disciplined, heartfelt rendering of music. It serves as a cultural bridge, connecting diverse traditions and generations. Children trained at the ashram's music academy, visitors from distant lands, senior disciples, and revered masters all find their place here in a shared atmosphere of reverence and learning. In an age where the arts often chase popularity and spectacle, the Nāda Mandapa quietly upholds the purity of purpose that music once held in ancient India—as a path to self-realization and as an offering to the Divine. Under Sri Swamiji's tireless guidance, it continues to be a space where music is not merely heard—it is felt, absorbed, and lived.

I would now come to Sri Datta Venkateshwara Temple, which is a spiritual bridge across traditions. Also in Mysuru Ashram is the beautifully crafted Sri Datta Venkateshwara Temple—a fusion of divine grace and spiritual innovation. Here, Lord Venkateshwara is worshipped with the deep wisdom of the Dattatreya tradition. This temple reflects Swamiji's inclusive approach—bringing together different streams of devotion into one harmonious flow. With its serene idol, symbolic carvings of Kamadhenu[68] and Kalpavriksha,[69] and powerful rituals, the temple offers much more than a religious experience. It becomes a spiritual training ground where values like patience, surrender, and selfless action are nurtured. Festivals and events held here are not just about ritual—they're about bringing people together, offering support, sharing joy, and reinforcing moral duty. This temple is a shining example of how ancient traditions can speak meaningfully to modern lives—reminding us that faith, when lived sincerely, can heal personal struggles and create stronger, more compassionate societies.

Now I come to Sri Karya Siddhi Hanuman Temple, Mysuru Ashram, the people's temple where prayers are fulfilled. Back in the heart of the ashram is another spiritual powerhouse—the Karya Siddhi Hanuman Temple. Here, the energy is almost tangible. Devotees arrive with worries, vows, and questions. They leave with peace, purpose, and stories of transformation. This is not just a temple of miracles. It is a sanctuary for the weary, a motivational space for the young, and a support system for those in crisis. Sri Swamiji designed it to be deeply personal yet publicly impactful. Daily rituals and group recitations of the Hanuman Chalisa create a rhythm of healing, while the temple's open atmosphere fosters a shared sense of belonging.

---

68. Kamadhenu is a divine, wish-fulfilling cow in Hindu mythology, believed to grant all desires and provide abundance, prosperity, and spiritual blessings. She is considered the mother of all cows and a symbol of selfless giving, often associated with sages, especially Vasishta.

69. Kalpavriksha is a mythical, celestial tree in Hindu, Jain, and Buddhist traditions that fulfills all wishes and desires of those who seek its blessings. It symbolizes abundance, divine grace, and the infinite generosity of nature or the Divine.

Sri Swamiji consecrated this magnificent 70-foot-tall Karya Siddhi Hanuman Statue in 2012 in the precincts of Sri Datta Venkateshwara Temple Complex at Sri Ganapathy Sachchidananda Ashram, Mysuru. This huge monolithic Hanuman statue is the tallest stone statue of Lord Hanuman in India. The temple has three Hanuman idols representing the three forms of Hanuman as per Ramayana—one being the tall monolithic statue, another for general worship and prayers, and the third idol is 'Pancha mukha Hanuman,' located underground.

What makes this temple so special is that it doesn't isolate people in private devotion. It unites them in public faith. The temple constantly encourages visitors to take the inner strength gained from Hanuman and turn it outward—into action, service, and kindness.

Temples That Serve, Inspire, and Uplift

Sri Ganapathy Sachchidananda Swamiji's temples—across continents and cultures—are not just about God. They are about people. Each one stands as a testament to how faith can be active, healing, inclusive, and socially uplifting. From giant idols that bring pride to diaspora communities to healing halls that use music as medicine to temples that raise compassionate citizens, Sri Swamiji's vision is clear: spirituality must serve humanity. These temples foster values like public service, cultural continuity, emotional resilience, and collective harmony. They inspire people to live better, help others, and find strength in something greater than themselves. In a divided world, they remind us of what truly matters—love, unity, and the courage to serve.

CHAPTER 16

The Miracle of Manifestation: Mass Chanting, Gita Recitations, and Sacred Constructions in the Era of Sri Ganapathy Sachchidananda Swamiji

Abstract

In a time when spirituality is often diluted by spectacle and devotion reduced to ritual, the life and works of Sri Ganapathy Sachchidananda Swamiji stand as luminous exceptions—testimonies to divine will manifesting through human action. This narrative explores the breathtaking miracles that unfolded through the large-scale chanting of the Hanuman Chalisa [70] *across continents, the mass recitations of the Bhagavad Gita*[71] *in sacred geographies like Kurukshetra and Chicago,*

70. The Hanuman Chalisa is a revered 40-verse hymn composed by the saint Tulsidas in Awadhi, extolling the strength, devotion, wisdom, and divine service of Lord Hanuman. Recited by millions for protection, courage, and spiritual upliftment, it encapsulates Hanuman's role as the ideal devotee and an embodiment of selfless bhakti

71. The Bhagavad Gita is a timeless philosophical dialogue between Lord Krishna and Prince Arjuna on the battlefield of Kurukshetra, addressing

and the conception and execution of monumental temple complexes and healing spaces like the Nāda Mandapa, Sri Datta Venkateshwara Temple, and the Karya Siddhi Hanuman temple in the Mysuru Ashrama. More than just events or constructions, these are spiritual phenomena—projects propelled not merely by funding or infrastructure but by a divine vision, relentless sankalpa, and collective surrender. Through these acts, Sri Swamiji not only redefined the possible but also set a new standard for devotional service and sacred achievement in the modern age.

~

It all began not merely with an idea, not even with a vision, but with divine intent. What Sri Ganapathy Sachchidananda Swamiji has achieved over the last few decades—both in India and abroad—defies easy explanation. For what mundane logic can account for the sheer scale, pace, and spiritual intensity of events and constructions that have come to define the Mysuru Ashrama and its ever-expanding global footprint? These are not just events or buildings. They are miracles—lived, witnessed, chanted, sung, and built in devotion.

Take, for instance, the mass chanting of the Hanuman Chalisa—a devotional event that would be monumental even if conducted in a single city. But this was no isolated effort. From Tenali to Hyderabad, Mysuru to Mumbai, from Dallas to New Jersey, the Hanuman Chalisa reverberated through the air, stirring minds and transforming hearts. In Dallas, USA, more than 1,28,000 Hanuman Chalisa recitations were completed in a 24-hour period during the Global Hanuman Chalisa Yagna, setting a Guinness World Record in 2015. The devotion was palpable, the energy electric. There was an invisible force

---

profound questions of duty, righteousness, and the nature of the self. As a spiritual cornerstone of Hindu thought, it synthesizes paths of devotion, knowledge, and action, offering guidance for ethical living and inner liberation.

uniting people across cultures, languages, and generations, and that force was the living current of Sri Swamiji's Sankalpa.

In India, these gatherings were nothing short of breathtaking. In Tenali, Hyderabad, Mysuru, and other cities, mass chants brought together thousands who echoed the Chalisa in perfect synchrony. One of the most iconic gatherings was the Hanuman Chalisa Maha Yagna in Mysuru in 2022, where over 60,000 devotees participated in person and many more online .

And then there were the *Bhagavad Gita* recitations—twice on the sacred battlefield of Kurukshetra. These were not symbolic events but actual large-scale recitations with devotees from across India and the world chanting all 700 verses of the Gita in the very place where Krishna revealed its truths to Arjuna. The first such event took place in 2013 and was followed by another in 2018, both presided over by Sri Swamiji . A similar spiritually-charged recitation occurred in Chicago in 2015, where the Gita was recited as part of the 'Gita Jayanti' celebrations during Sri Swamiji's US visit . Each of these events invoked the timeless message of dharma and inner transformation.

In Mysuru Ashrama, the *Bhagavad Gita* is not just a text—it is a lived ethos. Sri Swamiji's teachings are deeply rooted in the Gita's principles of detached action, inner calm, and steadfast faith. This spirit has materialized, quite literally, in the form of architectural and cultural marvels that have emerged from the ashrama's soil.

The construction of the Nāda Mandapa was a revolution in sacred architecture (described earlier). Dedicated to Nāda Chikitsa—healing through sound—it is a state-of-the-art musical and spiritual auditorium with over 2,000 seating capacity and designed with acoustic engineering excellence to enhance Sri Swamiji's therapeutic music concerts. Here, Raga Ragini Vidya blends seamlessly with spiritual healing, with Sri Swamiji's compositions using ancient ragas to soothe body and soul. Musicians of great repute consider it a privilege to render sangeet seva during Navaratri, Dattatreya Jayanti, Mahashivaratri and other festivals in Nāda Mandapa.

Equally astonishing is the Sri Datta Venkateshwara Temple, consecrated in 1999, whose architecture mirrors that of Tirumala while embodying the distinct vibrational energy of Datta Peetham. The temple, including the uniquely sculpted Garuda Vahanas and Pancha Mukhi[72] Hanuman, was completed on an accelerated timeline, backed not only by architectural precision but also by a divine blueprint that Sri Swamiji revealed during His meditative state.

How can one forget what rises as the stunning Karya Siddhi Hanuman Temple, where a 70-foot-tall Hanuman statue commands attention and reverence. Completed in 2012 and consecrated with a rare Hanuman Shakti Puja, the statue symbolizes the removal of obstacles and divine grace that ensures success in all endeavors. The Hanuman here is not only a murti but an energy field. His gaze seems to pierce through the devotee's fears and uncertainties. The larger 85-foot statue is located in Carapichaima, Trinidad, and was also installed by Sri Swamiji in 2003.

Behind each of these miracles was not a high-powered committee of consultants or a flurry of bureaucratic files. There was one mind, one sankalpa—that of Sri Swamiji. Volunteers, officials, and devotees found themselves swept up in this divine current. The fundraising was spontaneous; no appeals were

72. A five-faced manifestation. Hanuman in the east, Narasimha in the south, Garuda in the west, Varaha in the north, and Hayagreeva, upwards—each symbolizing distinct attributes such as courage, fearlessness, protection, strength, and wisdom. This form was assumed during the Ramayana to extinguish five lamps simultaneously and defeat the demon Ahiravana, thereby rescuing Bhagwan Ram and Lakshman from the netherworld.

necessary. People gave with joy, often anonymously, simply to be part of a sacred moment in history. The architectural planning, engineering, legal clearances, logistics—everything aligned as though the universe had decided that nothing would stand in the way.

Sri Swamiji did not merely build. He manifested. And He did it at a pace that left observers stunned. For in a world used to delays and complications, His projects moved with the rhythm of divine will—precise, unfaltering, and luminous.

The story of these divine manifestations is more than a chronicle of chanting and construction—it is a living testimony to the power of sankalpa shakti, of bhakti yoked to karma. In every mass Hanuman Chalisa chant, in every resounding verse of the Gita, and in every carved stone of the ashrama's sacred architecture, the invisible becomes visible, the ideal becomes real, and the impossible becomes routine. Sri Ganapathy Sachchidananda Swamiji has not merely inspired devotion; He has redefined what it means to live with devotion. His vision turned ordinary days into epochs and sacred spaces into portals of transformation. These are not just miracles of the past—they are blueprints for what is still to come. For with such divine leadership, the leela continues.

References

1. Guinness World Record for Hanuman Chalisa Chanting – SGS Hanuman Temple, Frisco, USA (2015): https://www.sgshanuman.org
2. Hanuman Chalisa Maha Yagna, Mysuru Ashrama Event Documentation (2022): https://www.dattapeetham.org
3. *Bhagavad Gita* Mass Recitation in Kurukshetra, Coverage (2013 & 2018): https://www.indiadivine.org/forums/topic/kurukshetra-saptaha-by-sri-ganapathy-sachchidananda-swamiji
4. Gita Jayanti Recitation – Chicago (2015): SGS International Center Events Archives

5. Nāda Mandapa Overview – Dattapeetham, Mysuru: https://www.dattapeetham.org/ashrama/nāda-mantapa
6. Sri Datta Venkateshwara Temple, Mysuru – Temple Records and Foundation Documentation: https://www.dattapeetham.org
7. Karya Siddhi Hanuman – Mysuru (36 ft) & Trinidad (85 ft): https://www.dattapeetham.org and https://www.sgshanuman.org/about-us/temples/trinidad-hanuman

EPILOGUE

The Soundless Sound, the Wordless Word

What began as a question—Who is Sri Ganapathy Sachchidananda Swamiji?—ends not with an answer but with a deep, resounding silence. Because the more you try to explain Him, the more you realize that He is the pause between thoughts, the space between sounds, and the presence behind the presence.

Through these pages, we have journeyed across continents, compositions, and consciousness. We have listened to the healing notes of ragas that touch the soul. We have watched lives change—from skeptics to believers, from pain to peace. We have walked through gardens of bonsai and aviaries of birds and emerged seeing the sacred pulse of life in every leaf and feather.

We have met a Master who plays a synthesizer like a veena, who conducts mass mantra chants like a cosmic conductor, who builds temples not just in stone but in hearts, breath, and silence. A sage who speaks in bhajans, teaches through music, and heals without needing to touch.

But if you ask me again, 'Who is Sri Swamiji?' I will now answer simply:

He is Presence.

He is Prana in motion.

He is Nāda Brahma walking this Earth.

He is that force that enters your life softly—perhaps as a bhajan on a cassette or a whisper from a loved one—and then changes everything.

This is not the end of the book. This is the beginning of your own journey.

Maybe it starts with a melody. Or a breath. Or just a sense that something greater is calling you—not outside, but from within. If this book has done its job, it hasn't just informed you about a saint. It has awakened a song inside you. A longing. A memory. A silence.

So now, close the book.

Open your ears.

Listen—not just to music, but to what comes after it.

That stillness.

That sweetness.

That soundless sound.

That is where He lives.

And that is where you'll find Him—Always.

In your breath.

In your silence.

In your soul.

Index